Style Me Vintage

Step-by-Step Retro Look Book

clothes * hair * make-up

Naomi Thompson is a stylist and personal shopper specialising in vintage fashion. She launched the first high tech on-line vintage shop, Vintage Secret, to immediate acknowledgement in the Guardian's 'What's Hot' list (second only to Ferragamo), quickly establishing a reputation for sourcing superb quality clothes at reasonable prices. In 2011 Naomi decided to put her expertise to good use and now is recognised as the UK's premier vintage personal shopper. She is passionate about finding good quality items at the right price, and believes that vintage is the way forward when it comes to creating your own style. www.vintagesecret.com

Belinda Hay is the founder of The Painted Lady, a unique boutique hair salon which specialises in vintage and contemporary colour, cuts and 'up do's' for ladies and gents. With over 12 years international expertise, Belinda's passion for all things vintage started at the tender age of five with an infatuation with Elvis Presley and 1950's fashion. After many years training in New Zealand and Australia, she worked for some of London's top hair salons before opening her own charismatic salon based in London's Shoreditch. She now creates signature cuts and styles beautifully tailored to clients seeking an 'of the moment' retro look. www.paintedlady.com

Katie Reynolds has been a hair and make-up artist for over 12 years, working in film, TV, music, commercials and fashion, with a celebrity client list. She founded The Powderpuff Girls in 2005 – a unique team of beauty professionals who provide a pampering service for events and parties. The girls also work at The Powder Room, a vintage-style beauty parlour open for everyone to come and experience their expertise. www.thepowderpuffgirls.com

Style Me Vintage

Step-by-Step Retro Look Book

clothes * hair * make-up

PAVILION

Contents

Introduction

Have you ever wanted to introduce vintage into your wardrobe, but felt unsure where to start?

Quite often people ask me where I buy my clothes and are surprised when I say, 'It's vintage!' Eschewing 'new' in favour of old, whether on a daily basis or just when you feel like it, is an option open to all and has surprising benefits. Curating your wardrobe from times beyond is like being your own designer and stylist rolled into one. Carefully picking and choosing items allows you to create your very own, unique style. Yes, this can be done with modern clothing, but the palette is limited. I cannot recommend enough the pleasure that comes from going against the grain. Wearing vintage can make you look individual and unique without slavishly following trends or spending money on expensive designer items. The ecological benefits are undeniable. The demand for vintage now means that fewer clothes are being condemned to the rag mill or dumped in landfills.

To help you on your way, you will find an introduction to the styles of the 1920s up to the 1980s. The twentieth century saw the dawn of modern tailoring; no other century has seen such a drastic shift in women's wear. These silhouettes and shapes are still being emulated, and will be for decades to come. You will not find any gimmicky looks here. Each outfit has been carefully selected for its reference points, focusing on a number of factors such as silhouette, print, and hemline, so that you can take this knowledge with you when searching for the perfect vintage outfit. This book does not seek to be a finite textbook guide to the rich tapestry of twentieth-century fashion; instead, it aims to hold your hand and gently guide you in the right direction.

Good classic vintage style is timeless. The looks from these decades are completely wearable today. It doesn't matter if you want to recreate an entire look or mix and match your favourite items from each decade. There is no right or wrong, just lots of fun creating your own vintage style. It may seem daunting at first – but as you build your collection, you will learn what to look for and what to avoid; and before you know it, you will know what is right for you. Many of my personal shopping clients find that, once they know about vintage cuts and shapes, they discover more about their own shape and find it easier to buy modern clothes.

For me personally, wearing vintage was the natural conclusion of a childhood spent snooping around my maternal grandmother Margaret's house. She was a pioneer of the vintage movement and had been picking up beautiful yet 'unfashionable' cast-offs since the 1960s. My mother and aunties have also worn some of the most cherished items in my collection. Choose your pieces well and they can become heirlooms for generations to come. I love that every dress, every bag, every scarf has a story that it would tell, if only it were able, and that I'm adding a chapter to that story. No modern item has ever made me feel as elegant or unique as a vintage one. Quite simply, vintage has magic. So if, like me, you like to wear clothes to feel creative and expressive, then vintage is for you. I promise that, with a little help, you will be turning heads in no time at all.

Whatever your reason for choosing to wear or explore vintage, I hope this book helps you find that special feeling. Who knows what hidden treasures are still out there to be discovered and enjoyed once more? Don't forget, life is too short for boring clothes.

Naomi

What is 'vintage'?

There has long been a debate on what constitutes 'vintage'. Purists would say that 'vintage' is pre-1960, and post-1960 is 'retro'. With the increase in popularity of old fashions, it has become apparent that designs from all the decades covered in this book are worthy of collecting and wearing. A good example of this is clothes from the 1980s. Whilst there are still many lingering horrors from that decade, which we will not be covering here (shell suits, anyone?), the Hervé Léger Bandeau dress is suddenly one of the most sought-after dresses of yonder and can command huge sums. Don't forget that the clothes of the last 30 years will be tomorrow's collectables, so it's worth looking out for good quality, iconic items now.

Quick guide to dating vintage

Learning to date vintage is like learning a language. After a good while of looking at many styles, stitches and patterns, buttons and prints, it just clicks. I promise you it does and is a most satisfying moment. From that point on, you can shop safe in the knowledge that you know what you are buying. Once in a while, an oddity will appear. I once saw a dress with wide tapered bell sleeves and a Celia Birtwell-like pattern. It screamed of the 70s and, in particular, the style of Ossie Clark. All the evidence indicated that it was, in fact, late 1930s. It's an amazing moment when you discover a one-off design that is far before its time. Just imagine the type of gal who would have worn or created such a dress.

There are no hard-and-fast rules for dating vintage, and it is often the source of debate amongst even the most seasoned connoisseurs. It's not uncommon to see a 30s print on a 40s dress, or an older frock with the metal zip replaced. There are always exceptions. It's a combination of the tips opposite and your own developing knowledge that will help to date your finds.

Left: When trying to date vintage clothing, collar shapes and button styles are always a good indicator of era.

1950s and earlier

How does it fasten? Is there a zip? If so, it should be metal. Poppers, hooks and eyes as the only fastener are a good indicator of early 20th century clothing.

Is the label embroidered or in a swirly font? Are the corners folded down where it has been sewn on?

Shoulder pads? Should be small, neat and fairly rigid.

Does it have a bra strap holder? (This is a small poppered ribbon to keep your bra in place between the shoulder and the dress fabric. It is also a sign of quality.)

Has the hem been hand-stitched? Is there a good length of material folded over?

Does it feel old? If it looks too new, it probably is. Trust your instincts.

Post-1950s

Is the zip plastic?

Does it have a care or washing instruction label?

Shoulder pads? May be large, spongy and generally not incorporated.

Does it have a size label?

Is it elasticated?

Have a good look at the inner seams. Are they over-locked? This only became common after the 1960s.

Developing your own style

Don't forget this is about fun! Unless you are trying to be purist, there are no rules. This is not prescribed high street fashion; it's your very own opportunity to build your own style.

When I take people shopping, I never ask their size or age beforehand. There is no need, as I believe that vintage really can be for everyone. You may be looking for a whole new outfit or simply the romance of an old scarf to tie onto a handbag. Please don't think that you are the wrong age or shape. This is not just a young thin woman's game – every age and shape can get in on the scene.

As I said, there are no rules unless you are trying to be a re-enactor – and, frankly, that is not about having fun with your style! Even the most hardcore purists I know like to mix reproduction with genuine vintage, and even the odd bit of high street. There are many good reproduction companies out there – and repro clothes and shoes also feature in this book.

So with that in mind, do remember: the iconic look of one decade quite often followed in to the next as the trends of the younger generations trickled down and became mainstream. Fashions always come in cycles. In the 60s, there was a 20s revival, which can be seen in the short layered dresses and Lolita-like styles. In the 70s, there was a trend for 30s cuts. In the 80s, the 40s can be seen in the resurrection of peplums and shoulder pads. Equally the

"Now is the most exciting time in fashion. Women are controlling their destiny now, the consumer is more knowledgeable, and I have to be better every single day." Oscar de la Renta

50s was back in fashion that same decade with full skirts and large florals. As Celia Birtwell once said, 'Nothing is new, really.'

Laver's Law of Fashionable Design (developed by noted costume historian James Laver) illustrates quite nicely why certain trends and fashion come back around. In fact, it has almost been 50 years since the first ever trend for 'vintage clothing' as we know it.

Laver's Law
10 years before – indecent
5 years before – shameless
One year before – daring
In fashion – smart
One year after – dowdy
10 years after – hideous
20 years after – ridiculous
30 years after – amusing
50 years after – quaint
70 years after – charming
100 years after – romantic
150 years after – beautiful

Never throw out a classic
(this list is according to my grandmother Margaret)

Polka dots

Leopard print

Tartan

Tweed

"The truly fashionable are beyond fashion." Cecil Beaton

Top tips for buying vintage

'Vintage' for me does exactly what it says on the tin. It's not just old or second-hand but a synonym for quality and durability – which may sound a little boring, but these are important factors when buying vintage from which you actually want to get some wear. It's very easy to fall in love with a shape or pattern and feel the need to snap it up instantly, but remember to take a deep breath, contain the excitement, and make sure you follow these essential tips when buying vintage clothes.

• Be prepared. Arm yourself with garments that are easy to get out of; something you can slip on and off without fuss – my favourite uniform for vintage shopping is a button-down dress. Wear minimal make-up. Many vintage garments do up at the side and have to go over your head, rather than over your hips, so whilst its tempting to don a red lippy to get into the spirit of things, it's best not to smear it all over the neck of a yellow 50s frock. You won't be judged in a shop for not looking the part.

• Always hold garments up to the light. Have you noticed how dark vintage shops can be? Well, it's not always intentional (they can just be cluttered places), but it sure does make it harder to spot flaws. By holding it up to the light you can instantly see any holes or repairs. The light will also shine through any patches where the fabric has become too thin and delicate. With woolen garments, check the elbows to make sure there is not excessive wear.

• Always check the armpits. As far as I am concerned, this is Number One in terms of importance; I don't know why it took me so long to do this automatically! Before the days of deodorant, sweat had a habit of damaging fabric due to the acidic qualities of perspiration. They may say horses sweat and ladies glow, but I have seen some amazing dresses (at amazing prices) ruined by sweat marks. Bad examples have a yellowy-green tinge. It can also cause the fabric to shred or a pattern to fade. Some dresses contain built-in sweat pads, similar to a shoulder pad; these can be easily removed without changing the shape of a garment.

• Look at the fastenings. Double-check that none of the buttons are missing and the zips are working properly. This may seem like a no-brainer, but all too often I've gotten home only to discover that a crucial covered button has fallen off or a zip is faulty. Key areas to check fastenings are around the neck line where small buttons may be hidden under a collar, and also around the cuffs. Whilst you are there, make sure the belt is still attached. If there are belt loops and no belt, it's OK to ask for a small discount because the garment is no longer complete.

• Shop with your hands. The best indicator of the quality of a garment is how it feels: is it silk or a bobbly synthetic? Is the twill soft or rough? This will help you identify the difference in quality between two similar dresses or suits of the same cut.

• Talk to the sales assistants. Don't be too proud to ask for advice in a shop, especially if you are looking for era-specific garments. This will speed up the learning process and before long you will be having a friendly debate on the age of a frock. Good shopkeepers should know their stock inside out and quite often they will keep special pieces behind for the right customer. It's also good to develop a relationship with the vendor, as they will start to look out for garments in your size and style. Most vintage sellers are passionate about what they do and are happy to talk to customers about stock, sizes and fair pricing.

• Go for the best you can afford. Resist the temptation to buy in bulk. Despite years of collecting for the sake of it, I now wish I had stuck to buying garments that were 100% wearable and in my size. My repairs bag is huge and you can't 'rescue' everything. The less you buy, the more you can spend on those show-stopping items!

- Shop for your body. Buy garments that fit, that you can move in, and don't be tempted to try and pour yourself into something too small. Whilst shapewear can make a difference (see page 94), you will only end up damaging the garment by splitting the fabric or popping the zip. Style and elegance is not about being a size 8; it is first and foremost about looking fabulous!

- Don't pay any attention to sizes on labels. Sizing is completely different nowadays, and if there is a size label I'm afraid the best option is to ignore it. To give you an example, I am an 8 but fit an 80s 10, a 60s/70s 12 and a 50s 14. Now, is this because women were smaller or are current brands changing sizes to make us feel better about ourselves? This has not yet been answered, and if you are interested in finding out more read up on Vanity Sizing. Gemma Seager, who writes the Retro Chick blog, is considered to be the industry expert.

- Always check the bottom of shoes. More often than not, a heel tip will be missing. Check the leather around the buckle and strap for signs of wear and tear. If a leather strap looks cracked, it may break off easily. Make sure the shoe is not too bendy and will hold your weight – this can be achieved only by trying it on. In some cases the shoe's sole can be reinforced, but this can be costly. Avoid shoes where the leather has stiffened, as they will be uncomfortable to wear.

- Don't be tempted by garments that need altering above and beyond a simple strap shortening or a dropped hem. Scant few alteration shops will do it justice and if the fabric is raw, frayed or thin, it may not last even one cold wash!

- Try to avoid buying items that are 'on trend'. I guarantee that you will be paying more than the item is worth. You will be buying into a fad at an inflated price that will lose its value next season. Buy what *you* like.

• *Don't* be scared to try anything on. If you like it on the hanger, then chances are you will like it on you, but you also shouldn't shy away from the bizarre; sometimes a hanger can't convey an item's true potential, so get it on your body – what's the worst that could happen? As a vintage personal shopper, this has been the most rewarding element of what I do. If I got a pound every time a customer reluctantly tried on a garment which turned out to be amazing, then I could probably retire! Have fun, expect the unexpected and shop with an open mind, as you never know what may turn up.

Vintage Shopping Kit List

A tape measure. With this and a good knowledge of your own measurements, you will save yourself a lot of stress finding changing rooms and squeezing into and out of too small items.

A wide belt to try things on with – dresses can look completely different once they are synched in.

A handbag with a strap to help free up your hands and avoid having to put things down. (I've put things down before, not realised and then seen them sporting a price tag on my next visit!)

A smile – it helps with discounts!

The Looks

The 1920s

"Fashion is not something that exists in dresses only. Fashion is in the sky, in the street, fashion has to do with ideas, the way we live, what is happening." Coco Chanel

The 1920s saw the dawn of style over dictated fashion. The end of the First World War in 1918 brought with it changes that liberated women and led them to rebel against the restrictions of corsetry and modest Edwardian values. Clothing became functional; silhouettes were less exaggerated, yet retained sophistication. As the 20s progressed hemlines crept up to the knee for the first time in history.

Day look shopping list

- Dropped waist lines
- Cloche hats
- Lace-up ankle boots
- Narrow pleated skirts
- Simple jersey knits
- Coloured opaque stockings
- Long tie-collars
- Calf-length hemlines
- Wrapover coats that secure with a single fastening
- Rounded shoes

Evening look shopping list

- Long ropes of pearls or glass beads
- Sheer, often sequinned dresses
- Enamelled or gilded chain-mail bags
- Seed pearl clutches
- Handkerchief hemlines (shorter linings and longer sheer overskirts)
- Bare gloveless arms
- Flesh and soft pastel stockings
- Ornate shoes with Louis heels
- Exotic headdresses and headbands

Main shapes, looks and influences

During the war of the preceeding decade many women had taken up work, and clothing changed to afford greater practicality. Women vastly outnumbered men, and attitudes changed completely from 'dutiful' to 'laissez faire'. The atrocities of war had given people a sense of mortality. Living for the moment became the lifestyle choice of this decade.

Whereas before the 20s the emphasis had been on minimising the waist and accentuating the cleavage, women were now inclined to wear unstructured, shorter dresses that skimmed the hips and flattened the chest. This silhouette is applicable throughout the 20s, for both day and eveningwear. The look was a sleek and slender silhouette, quite flat and boyish. The drop waist was the main feature of the 20s and created a longer less feminine frame. Sashes were popular on day dresses and could be worn loosely around the hips or draped over the shoulder (see page 29). The big revolution, however, was that a visible ankle was now not only socially acceptable but fashionable.

As dress shapes became simpler so did the manufacturing process. Butterick, the pattern company launched in 1863, introduced the first pattern instruction sheet, 'the Deltor', which removed the need to be an experienced dressmaker. This, combined with simple shapes, enabled women to make their own clothes. Designer patterns became popular in women's magazines, often emulating Chanel or Lanvin designs. These garments were also easier to wash and repair.

Coats buttoned up really low, often with one single fastening. Opera coats became popular, but the big trend was a velvet Devoré evening coat, trimmed with luxurious fur such as mink or sable.

Hats changed from wide-brimmed floral extravaganzas to daintier cloches and smaller hats to fit in with the new streamlined silhouette.

The opening of Tutankhamen's tomb launched Egyptomania, especially in accessories. Handbags, shoes and cigarette cases were all adored with the hieroglyphics discovered in 1923. Chain-mail bags peaked in popularity in the Edwardian era and were used throughout the 20s. Seed pearl bags were all the rage and featured a small side strap, commonly thought to be for slipping your hand though, but which was, in fact, to secure your gloves. This was then carried much like a clutch.

Coco Chanel designed her little black dress in 1926, known as the 'Model T' after Henry Ford's popular car. She was arguably the most important influence of this decade. At the forefront of female emancipation, she introduced simply cut garments influenced by men's designs, such as wide trousers (though still very avant-garde for women), long jumpers and, crucially, women's tailoring.

Far left: Velvet opera coat with balloon sleeves in a geometric print.

Above left: Boudoir dolls were reportedly used as a fashion accessory by those who sought to emulate the childlike look.

Above right: A selection of cloche hats and ornate hat pins.

Below: Earlier accessories can still complete a 20s look, such as hair combs and mesh bags.

Right: 'Modern' accessories of the day included celluloid arm bangles and seed pearl clutch bags.

Opposite: This 20s dress is relatively long but has a daring side-split.

Top 20s tip
Avoid the clichéd look of long gloves and a hair feather and instead go for a simple gold head band draped around the forehead and metres of looped glass beads.

What was new?

As the decade progressed a new poster girl for excess and indulgence emerged around 1926: The Flapper. The term 'flapper' has roots going right back to the 17th century and referred to a young and vivacious girl. The 1920 film *The Flapper* bought the word into popular culture. The name reflected a somewhat juvenile desire not to grow up. This gal was all about all having fun: drinking, smoking, misbehaving in public and dancing outrageously until the small hours. To go with this brazen behaviour, Flapper attire was more revealing than ever before in history. Dresses were generally sleeveless and fabrics were so fine they bordered on sheer. They were usually lavishly embroidered with sequins and glass beads. Few have survived today as the early sequin was made of gelatine, which had a tendency to melt. Towards the end of the 20s, the streamlined silhouette remained but the detailing became simpler.

It was at this point in the mid-20s (and not before) that the knee briefly appeared. Hemlines were shorter than ever and often trimmed with rows of beaded tassels. There is much debate about how much knee was actually shown. This depended on the cut of the dress: some fell below the knee, but exposed the thigh by a side-split, others just skimmed the knee.

Flamboyant use of make-up added to the Lolita effect: heavy ringed eye make-up, doll-like eyebrows, and scarlet lipstick on a pale face. Hair also underwent a dramatic transformation.

Whilst it was still popular to have it curled and pinned up, a new shorter style appeared: the Bob. This boyish crop symbolised the cutting away of Edwardian sensibilities. Finger waves were also popular and could be combined with a new shorter 'do.

The combination of childish innocence and open sexuality caused scandal amongst the establishment. The Flappers didn't really care; this was the Jazz age and and they were determined to celebrate their own youth.

Informal Looks

On the right, Teowa is wearing a drop-waisted 20s day dress with a shoulder sash (this could also be worn as a loose belt). Note the pleated skirt and embroidered detailing. She is also wearing typical 20s satin court shoes edged in gold leather. The black dress on the left shows a style that would have been worn by an older woman. It follows the fashionable straight lines and pleats of the decade, but is less risqué.

A Flapper Look

Annie is wearing a 20s gold sequinned evening dress. The shoulder straps consist of strands of glass beads and the side slits are are decorated with tasselled roundels. This sandal style of shoe was more popular in the 30s, but can be made to work with a 20s outfit. A classic 20s shoe would have had been similar, but with a closed toe. The look is finished off by celluloid arm bangles, an ostrich feather hair piece and a late Edwardian chain bag.

The 1930s

"When a woman smiles, then her dress should smile too."

Madame Vionnet

The 1930s saw the beginning of social unrest on both sides of the pond. The Great Depression hit the United States and World War II started in Europe. Cinema provided much-needed escapism. The gamine playfulness of the last decade was pushed aside and a new age of strong feminine dressing swept in. Clothes became even more practical, in the form of well-tailored suits, or they became outrageously glamorous as epitomised by the sirens of the silver screen. The clothes of the 30s were cut to suit the female body: instead of trying to change the silhouette, they celebrated the female physique. Curves were definitely back in fashion.

Day look shopping list

- Calf-length hemlines
- Gored, A-line skirts (flaring panels)
- Shawl collars
- Top-stitching, contrast fabric insertions, large buttons.
- Neckline details such as a pleated yoke, ruffled jabot, bow or Peter Pan collar done up high
- Cap or puff sleeves
- Tilt hats – worn tipped to the side and adorned by bows, feathers or brooches
- Muted earthy tones of mustard, jade and reddish brown
- T-bar stacked heels
- Lace-up ankle shoes with a rounded toe
- Wide-brimmed straw hats with a low crown (for summer)

Evening look shopping list

- Full length, cut on the bias and draped
- Dark velvets in jewel tones
- Deep V-necks, front and back
- Full-length skirts
- Scalloped edges
- Fishtail skirts
- Matching or integral belts with a carved celluloid or paste clasp
- Art Deco cut jewels
- Jackets with a nod to Leg o' Mutton sleeves

Main shapes, looks and influences

The general look for both day and evening was sleek. Day skirts and dresses often included pleated or inserted panels called godets, starting below the knee or just above the hemline. The emphasis was on detail, such as buttons, lace, bows. Utter chic and femininity was combined with functionality and simplicity.

This decade also saw the first widespread use of regenerated fibres such as rayon, which was first known as art silk. It was used as a cheaper substitute for both day and eveningwear.

By the mid-1930s, empire lines became popular accompanied by short jackets or capelets. Dresses were cut with a fitted yoke and a strong emphasis on the shoulders, which paved the way for the shoulder pads of the 1940s. The print that epitomises this era for me is floral pastels contrasted with black, for both day and evening wear.

Evening dresses became quite daring. Some were made to be worn bra-less, such as Molyneux's trend for white backless slip dresses, a look completed by a fur draped over the shoulders, or a velvet Opera coat with a fur trim.

The sandal as we know it appeared in the 30s. Ferregamo, shoe maker to the stars, invented the wedge heel in 1936 to combine comfort and style. The T-bar was popular for day and evening shoes. Evening shoes were often made of satin, trimmed with silver or gold kid leather, and accented with rhinestone buckles.

What is a bias cut?

The 'bias' cut is first and foremost a dressmaking technique that involves cutting the fabric against the grain. A bias cut dress is quite often characterised by V-shape panels below the bust line.

So how is it done? The pattern pieces are first cut against the grain and then sewn across the grain of the fabric. This allows it to drape elegantly whatever your shape or size. This is a clever trick to give horizontal stretch to inelastic fabrics. It flatters and enhances the contours of one's physique without being too tight and appearing lumpy. This cut is often accompanied by a long skirt for a beautiful willowy look.

Above: Housecoats/dresses became popular in the 30s for the middle classes and would be worn for lounging, not cleaning, as is often the misconception. Far from being dowdy, they were beautifully made as outerwear. Kezia is wearing a housedress with Greek key motif and 'fruit salad' coloured glass earrings.

Far Left: Gemma is wearing an early 1930s calf-length silk dress with a large bow-effect collar, balloon sleeves and cummerbund-style belt. Its straight cut with smooth lines creates a long, lean silhouette.

Three influential designers of the 30s were Coco Chanel (again), Vionnet and Elsa Schiaparelli. Madame Vionnet, who had trained at the famed Callot Soeurs couture house in Paris, was responsible for many of the well known shapes that are associated with eveningwear of the 1930s. She was renowned for her drapery and popularised halter necks and the bias cut.

The art of Surrealism extended its influence into the worlds of textiles, fashion and interiors. Schiaparelli collaborated with many of her friends, including Salvador Dali, basing her humorous inventions, such as the Tear Dress, on their work. This went against the grain of 'grown-up' fashions. She also invented Shocking Pink and her tailoring was an antidote to the formality and drapery of Madame Vionnet.

What was new?

Sportswear slowly crept in via Chanel in the late 1920s, but became fashionable in its own right in the 1930s. Lacoste began in 1933 and Fred Perry shot to fame in the 1930s with his consecutive Wimbledon wins. The 30s in general promoted 'the body beautiful' and a toned and lean shape. Exercise activities, such as group aerobics, were encouraged. Swimming, tennis and cycling were also hugely popular and clothing ranges were developed with this in mind. Holiday time for workers became a mandatory requirement, which meant beach holidays increased in popularity. Play suits, pyjama suits and all sorts of novel leisurewear inventions were seen on the sandy shores of Britain.

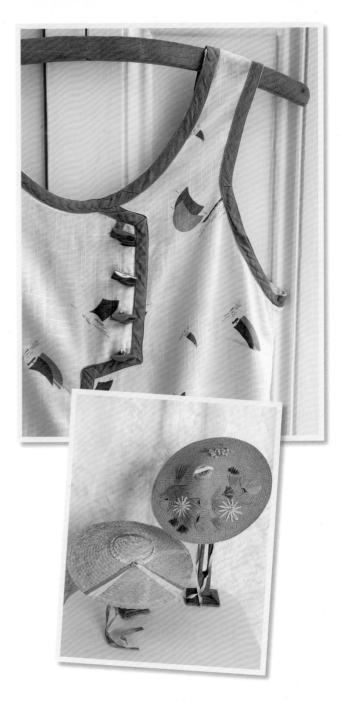

Top tip to date a 1930s dress

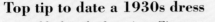

Take a good look at the fastenings. Zips were not commonly used in women's wear as they were considered unreliable, and therefore prone to immodesty. Dresses mainly fastened via hooks and eyes, or poppers (press studs), on the side seam, or via rouleau loops and small covered buttons down the back.

Near right: Pairs of deco clips were used for shoes and dresses and could be mounted as brooches. Crocheted gloves were easy to make at home.

Far right: Celluloid diamante brooches were popular accessories. Country pursuits influenced daytime accessories as seen in this duck brooch and glass bird necklace.

Opposite top: Leisure- and sportswear became popular in the 30s, as seen in this beach dress with sailing motif and early plastic toggle buttons.

Opposite below: Low-brimmed 30s straw hats with ribbon ties.

Daytime Look

Gemma is wearing a repro-1930s suit from Puttin' on the Ritz with asymmetric pleat detailing on the skirt and a curved collar to the jacket. The skirt is a classic mid-calf-length. On the jacket there's a single button fastening, which was very in vogue. The original 1930s blouse is made from rayon crêpe, in chocolate brown with orange print, and features a 'jabot' (neck ruffle) with a Bakelite button. Her outfit is finished off with a felt hat and glacé leather gloves.

Evening Look

Kezia is wearing a full length, satin back crêpe evening dress, cut on the bias with a shirred bodice and waterfall beading. She carries an ostrich feather fan and white faux fox stole, and long elegant silver cigarette holder. Smoking was socially acceptable, and even encouraged. Although we cannot see it from this angle, the dress features a low V-back, which is very characteristic of a 30s evening look.

The 1940s

"Nothing is so dangerous as being too modern; one is apt to grow old-fashioned quite suddenly." Oscar Wilde

By the 1940s, war had broken out across Europe. Fashion was no longer the primary concern, but standards were there to be maintained. Raw materials such as cloth were in short supply and much of the traditional labour had left to fight. Rather than buying 'new', women were encouraged to 'make do and mend'. Many shapes of the 30s were simplified to suit the demands of the times. Whilst fabric was in short supply, necks and backs were covered up and modesty prevailed once more.

Day look shopping list

- Tweed
- Headscarves
- Chunky synthetic jewellery
- Peplums
- Seamed stockings
- Single-breasted jackets
- Shoulder pads
- Housecoats, aprons and pinnies
- Mah-Jong bracelets
- Suits

Evening look shopping list

- Most evening dresses were adapted from pre-war dresses, so there is a genuine crossover in styles
- Platform-soled shoes with or without a peep toe
- Crêpe dresses
- Cordé bags
- Carved Bakelite jewellery
- Furs

Main shapes, looks and influences

A typical wartime look was a prim dark crêpe dress adorned by whatever pretty embellishments were available. Wartime garments tend to be darker and less patterned, as people refashioned old fabrics by dyeing them. Sequins came under the Utility Scheme and Civilian Clothing Order, which forbade their use. Even if these rulings hadn't been in place they would have been hugely difficult to get hold of as the best makers were in occupied Europe. There are still some examples of utility clothing which are embroidered with sequins. There is evidence that the ruling was relaxed later on in the decade, which is why some sequin-embellished garments are seen bearing the CC41 label.

It wasn't all doom and gloom. British clothing company Jacqmar was producing bright propaganda scarves as a morale-boosting exercise, and the US continued to manufacture brightly coloured printed garments such as Swirl pinafore dresses, which were favoured by housewives.

This was the decade that trousers became acceptable, even featuring on the front cover of US *Vogue* in May 1941! Initially adopted by women working in factories, they were practical, which made them a desirable garment. High-waisted and wide-legged, they were often described as slacks.

Unlike other clothing, hats were not rationed, though snoods and head scarves became very popular as they combined the key themes of the 40s: fashion and practicality.

The signature 40s look of narrow hips and wide shoulders can be seen on Lisa on page 49. Suits shifted to a boxier jacket with less fabric in the length. The shoulder was lengthened by the arrival of the mighty shoulder pad (not an 80s invention as many still think).

Left: Fleur is wearing Heyday swing trousers, a hand-knitted-from-vintage-pattern bolero, a Heyday Olivia blouse and white Re-mix vintage wedges, finished off with a mah-jong bracelet and a white snood.

Opposite: Cordé bags are very collectable. Suede peep-toe wedges can work well for a day or evening look.

Above left: A stocking repair kit. Stockings were popular but scarce. American GIs would bring with them highly sought-after nylons, but in the absence of anything better, gravy browning was applied to the legs and a seam was pencilled on to replicate a fully fashioned stocking.

Above right: A UK Utility label, designed by Reginald Shipps, resembled two opened-mouth Pac Men.

Right: Hats were not rationed during the war though many were adapted from much older styles.

Far right: Embellishments were often recycled from the 30s.

What was new?

In 1941 rationing was introduced to the UK. Rather than restricting the distribution of clothing, the aim was to ensure equal access to goods and products. All new clothing produced had to be purchased with coupons. The Utility label was a sign of government-approved quality. Not all clothing was Utility, but all manufacturers were expected to follow austerity measures. The point was practicality. This stamped its mark on fashions of the decade, as shapes changed in accordance with ration allowances. Jackets became shorter and boxier, and often lacked a collar or pockets to save on materials. Hemlines rose to the knee (but not above), buttons went down to 2 or 3 and pleats were definitely out in the UK. The less raw materials used, the better. Utilitywares were hard wearing items, built to last and appeared in a surprising number of ranges and colours. It continued throughout the decade, ending only in 1952.

The fashion houses of Paris launched into production once more in 1945 at the end of the war and a new era of long overdue creativity sprang into life. The mundane came to a sharp end with the unveiling of Christian Dior's ultra-feminine first collection in 1947. Declared by *Harpers Bazaar's* Carmel Snow as 'the New Look' (it was actually called the Corolle Line), it featured the iconic Bar suit, which went on to develop the look of the 50s. During the war, fashion had pretty much stood still. Clothing now became a pleasure once again.

Top 40s tip
For a really authentic 40s look, unearth a patriotic flag brooch or propaganda scarf. Many countries produced their own.

Formal Look

Lisa is wearing a late-40s shantung-effect suit with diamanté button detail and a Hattie Carnegie early-40s sculptural velvet hat with velvet-tipped hat pin. She also wears 40s screw-back black enamel and diamante earings, black suede with rosette detail shoes and a black suede bag.

Informal Look

Fleur is wearing a vintage novelty print Swirl wrap dress, red shoes from Re-mix Vintage Shoes, What Katie Did seamed stockings and plenty of vintage bangles.

49

The 1950s

"Be daring, be different, be impractical, be anything that will assert integrity of purpose and imaginative vision against the play-it-safers, the creatures of the commonplace, the slaves of the ordinary." Cecil Beaton

The 1950s was a decade of reawakening, rebellion, discovery and progress. Musical genres of the previous decade morphed into new crazes, including doo-wop, bebop, cool jazz, blues and notably the emergence of Rock 'n' Roll; a musical genre that would probably produce some of the greatest icons of the decade or, even, century. In Movie Land, Marilyn gave us curves, and the rebirth of European cinema after the oppression of the war brought us smouldering sirens like Sophia Loren. The shape of the 50s was the contrast of a tiny waist with rounded hips in a pencil or a full skirt. This was truly the decade of the hourglass figure.

Horrockses

Day look shopping list

- Beaded cardigans
- Nipped-in waistlines
- ¾-length sleeves on jackets
- Shelf busts (darted bust lines)
- Cat's eye sunglasses
- Novelty prints and jewellery
- Box handbags
- Bright floral patterns
- Circle skirts
- Tie blouses
- Bobby socks
- Saddle shoes
- Short gloves

Evening look shopping list

- Full skirts
- Long gloves
- Brocade
- Modern synthetics
- Triple rows of pearls, worn choker-style
- Rhinestone paste clip-on earings
- Boned strapless bodices
- Chiffon/Organza
- Layers of petticoats
- Small clutch bags with ornate clasps
- Fur stole or wrap

Main shapes, looks and influences

The 1950s was a time of immense change. Europe was recovering from the devastating effects of World War II with rationing continuing into the early 50s. The world saw great shifts in political attitudes, with the growing threat of communism, fear of nuclear weapons and the Korean War. Great advances in technology saw the beginnings of the Space Race and the Atomic Era, both strong influences on design. For the first time, popular culture focused on 'teenagers', a new subculture whose fashion styles, music choices and cultural influences dominated the decade.

The style associated with the 50s began with Dior's Corolle Line of 1947. The look was characterised by a structured jacket, tiny waist and full skirt. This came to represent the iconic feminine shape of the 1950s. Even today this silhouette is much copied. The shape continued to be worn throughout the 1950s and into the early 1960s, within the framework of dresses and coats alike. Think big belted jackets, and shirtwaster dresses with a full skirt and big collar.

Magazines mixed photography with traditional sketches. It was the dawn of the golden age of fashion photography. For the first time, fashion photographers became stars.

Another great introduction during this era, and what I believe to be one of the most important of the century, is the wearing of jeans and denim as a casual and acceptable daytime look for

men and women. Jeans were first worn in the early twentieth century but only as sturdy work wear. No respectable, well-dressed individual would be seen in them outside of this context. This changed with their rebirth as a fashion staple in the 1950s. Seen as a rebellious item – think James Dean or Teddy Girls – they made a statement and have continued to play a large part in our wardrobes today. To create a 50s look, go for indigo denim with a high waist and turn-ups.

What I love about the 1950s is the bold and fantastic use of print. Fabric designers, such as Lucienne Day and Marian Mahler, had begun to use the most fabulous shapes and colours in textile production. Novelty prints abounded (see fabric on pages 92–3). In the United States, dachshunds and poodles were embroidered and printed onto fabrics. Globally, designs were influenced by the positive attitude towards the future of atomic energy and were widely used in clothing and homeware design.

Horrockses became one of the most respected and iconic companies of the decade, creating beautiful full-skirted frocks in a variety of coloured fruits, flowers and blooms.

The Festival of Britain in 1951 was a celebration of British Design and provided a showcase of post-war recovery. The design styles exhibited were the starting block for a decade of iconic design.

Above: Two examples of the poodle trend.

Opposite: Rachel is wearing a nautical cotton two-piece with a tapered bodice which sits over the skirt. Large pockets with a button detail are quite common on 50s frocks and reflect the increased availability of fabric. Jeni is wearing a pink candy-striped halterneck with a matching bolero jacket.

Souvenirwear and novelty jewellery were popular in the 50s. This painted basket bag would have come from Mexico. The box bag below, although Californian, depicts a scene from the springs of Mount Fuji. Cat's eye sunglasses came in many colours.

In the United Kingdom, Queen Elizabeth II was a source of inspiration for women. She was the first young monarch since Queen Victoria, and her ladylike style was copied up and down the country by women of all backgrounds. Her outfits were always finished with a brooch, gloves and bag.

Lucite became a popular material for the creation of the fashionable box-style handbags. These small, translucent creations were luxurious and expensive, but cheaper designs soon came onto the market.

Lucite was also a popular material for sexy, see-through shoes. The heel of these would often be carved and included jewelled decoration. The slip-on mule was another popular ladies shoe. Shoes became even higher and pointier than before with the stiletto heel reaching its thinnest.

The waist remained a big (or small!) feature throughout the decade, with jackets and dresses shaped accordingly, and the wider 'cinch' style belt introduced to accentuate feminine curves. Capri or cigarette pants (calf-length, slim-legged, high-waisted trousers) were popular and were often worn with a tight sweater. This sexy, rebellious style became known as the 'Sweater Girl' look, and this silhouette would, of course, be incomplete without a conical bra.

Right: This extravagant 50s ball gown is modelled in an ode to Cecil Beaton. It features 12 layers of cotton and tulle.

Top 50s tip

Contrary to popular belief, the 50s shape can suit everyone. A full, high-waisted skirt can hide a multitude of sins. A simple rule for an authentic 50s vintage look: Keep your hemlines just below the knee – never above. Providing the length is correct, it also elongates the calf and makes ankles appear slimmer.

Top 50s tip

Don't be tempted to wear a full petticoat or crinoline underskirt that sticks out past your hemline. This won't add to your 50s look.

Capri Pant Look

Jeni is wearing bright yellow capri pants with a tie waist. Her bark-cloth crop top with pom pom detailing evokes the Tiki style that became fashionable in the 1950s in both clothing and homeware. Her look is finished off with a chiffon headscarf, bamboo hooped earrings and wedge mules.

Full-skirted Look

Jeni is wearing a traditional homemade 50s floral cotton dress with a nipped-in waist, full skirt and cap sleeves. The dress features a 'collar' which cleverly folds down to form a squarer take on a sweetheart neckline. White mesh summer courts, plastic flower earrings and a parasol to shade her complexion complete the look.

59

The 1960s

'There's so much plastic in this culture that vinyl leopard skin is becoming an endangered synthetic.' Lily Tomlin

Pop music was exploding – from Beatlemania to the Rolling Stones. Boys wanted to be them, and women everywhere wanted to emulate their stylish girlfriends. The 60s left behind all the fuss and constraints of the 40s and 50s; youngsters were outgrowing the 'Make Do and Mend' generation and being frivolous and flirty. Women were more liberated than they had been before – and boy, did it show. Hemlines rose and rose and the miniskirt was born.

Day look shopping list

- Bib fronts
- Monochrome
- Mary Jane shoes
- Pilgrim shoes
- Tights (certainly not seamed stockings!)
- Vinyl accessories
- Trapeze bags
- Square/circular bangles
- Boots

Evening look shopping list

- Sequined mini dresses
- Short baby doll dresses
- Watteau backs (a single back panel that falls unbelted to the hem, like a train)
- Dress suits
- Tailoring
- Matching accessories

Main shapes, looks and influences

Skirt lengths got shorter and shorter throughout the 60s, but it was 1965 when the mini as we know it, sometimes 8 inches above the knee, was born. Mary Quant coined the name apparently in ode to the Mini car. It revolutionised fashion: it was something never seen before; it was bold and brash and it upset your parents. Most importantly, it was something that the average girl could and would wear. High fashion was no longer for the elite.

Lesley Hornby aka Twiggy, Jean Shrimpton and Marianne Faithful were the supermodels of their time. Girls could copy their looks without having to save up for months. The biggest contribution to this fashion revolution was the fact that clothes were so much cheaper to manufacture and distribute across the globe. Biba by Barbara Hulanicki launched in 1963, bringing fashion for the masses by introducing cheap clothing via mail order. She described her ranges as 'Auntie Colours' – blackish mulberries, blueberries, rusts and plums. Gone were the stuffy tailors and there was a big hello to the achingly trendy Kings Road boutiques in Chelsea and Carnaby Street in Soho, London.

The use of plastic was another defining feature. Vinyl (or PVC) was used for coats (especially macs, often with matching rain hats) and even mini dresses. It was also commonly used to make bright chunky jewellery. The demand for fast fashion saw the rise of mass-produced synthetic bags and shoes.

Left: Ladylike accessories and chunky plastic jewellery are very of this era. As are square circle bangles and earrings. If you want to avoid the white go-go boot look, any 60s outfit can be nicely finished off with a Mary Jane-style shoe.

Right: A heavily embellished rhinestone, pearl and bead mini dress.

Opposite top: A scarf tied to a bag can add a personal touch to an otherwise muted outfit.

Opposite below: Pilgrim shoes with a big buckle and flat heel. Wear with white tights for an elongated leg.

What was new?

London was the hub of youth culture and was the epitome of the Swinging Sixties. David Bailey's images of Jean Shrimpton are some of the most iconic images of all time. The film *Blow Up* was said to be based on him. Andy Warhol's pop art was influencing fashion. Amazing prints from Pucci sprung up, all with glorious colours, and weird and wonderful designs were created. Was it fashion or was it art? Some would say both.

The space race dominated the decade. Designers appropriated perceived elements of spacemens' suits – flashes of white, silver and cocoon-like headwear.

The 1960s cannot be talked about without mentioning its two biggest subcultures, the Mods and the Rockers. With motorcycles being the best alternative to the expensive motor car, youngsters were able to be mobile and express themselves in a whole new way. On one hand you had the dapper Modernist boys, who wore Italian bespoke suits and had sharp haircuts; the girls weren't far behind, with their stylish pencil skirts and cardigans. They danced to The Kinks and The Who, or American R&B. On the other hand you had the Rockers, who were less sophisticated in dress but had a very iconic look, combining leather jackets and denim. Both of these looks are still very much around today all over the globe, from Australia to Japan.

Top 60s tip

Look out for dress suits: a shift dress with matching fitted jacket. Wear together for a Jackie O look, or use as separates.

Informal Look

Alice wears a red and white bib front dress with statement collar. Note the very short skirt and a nod to flower power in its daisy trim. The look is finished with white Mary-Jane shoes and matching square bracelets.

Formal Look

Laura is wearing a Frank Russell for Mansfield coat and a belted two-tone minidress. Frank Russell was a young Jewish tailor from the East End of London who became the 'King of Coats' and sold in high-profile outlets such as Selfridges and Harrods. The cut and the style is very typical of the mid-60s. A white handbag and Pilgrim shoes complete the look.

The 1970s

'Over the years I have learned that what is important in a dress is the woman who is wearing it.' Yves Saint Laurent

The rise in air travel, combined with the newly accessible Spanish coast, encouraged holidays abroad. In the United States the Vietnam War had ended, and the new worry was the environment. Climate control had arrived and you could sit in a heated car without a coat. Clothing became multifunctional, moving seamlessly from day to night. Diane von Furstenberg created the simple jersey wrap dress, which could be worn to the office or on the dancefloor.

Day look shopping list

- Tank tops
- Prairie/peasant dresses
- Crochet waistcoats
- Broderie anglaise
- Fringed leather skirts
- Denim
- Polo necks
- Plaited or weaved belts
- Patchwork
- Safari suits
- Pussy bow blouses
- Wide lapels and collars
- Tunics
- Pinafores
- Capes

Evening look shopping list

- Mirror-tile belts
- Cropped, faux-fur jackets
- Lurex
- Low V-necks
- High ruffled necks
- Spaghetti straps
- Halter necks
- Jumpsuits
- Maxi skirts
- Glitter
- Asymmetric tops and dresses

Main shapes, looks and influences

Above and right: It's still pretty easy to find 70s accessories in charity shops. Look out for oversized sunglasses with a squarish frame and long strands of beads. The 70s saw a fondness for mixed-tone leather shoulder bags. Carved bangles were also popular.

The early 70s were all about personal creativity: fashions were either handcrafted, or made to look so. Macramé (woven coloured plastic or straw), crochet and patchwork were popular across the ages. Magazines such as *Over 21* produced a quarterly supplement, *Fashion Workshop*, which combined the latest styles with all the craft techniques needed to make a mirrored belt or knitted sweater.

In America, Bev Hillier's 1971 Art Deco Exhibition reignited a passion for the 30s, which extended to fashions. This is also, importantly, the beginning of the vintage trend as we know it, though it was still known then as 'second hand'. This wasn't recycling out of necessity; it was a lifestyle choice. 'Anything goes' was the attitude towards wearing past fashions and this new 'fad' had a fairly broad appeal.

These trends trickled up to the biggest designers of the day. Ossie Clark and Alice Pollock appropriated the best of 30s eveningwear and turned it into 70s daywear. The bias cut returned, though sleeves became exaggerated versions of their former incarnations. The empire line reappeared. Colours returned to a rich autumnal palette of deep purples, burnt oranges and greens in abstract or mixed floral patterns, though less psycadelic than the previous decade.

The teenage mini skirt trend of the 60s had become a mainstream fashion, worn by mothers and daughters alike. Two new hem lines were introduced: the Midi (A-line and calf length – another nod to the 30s) and the Maxi (a huge volumous creation that came at least to the ankle).

Jeans and trousers were flared, increasing to their largest in the mid-70s. As the decade came to a close, they had slimmed right down to the peg leg shape associated with the 80s, though the high waist remained.

Popular shoes were, of course, platforms, clogs and simple flat sandals from Scholls.

What was new?

In 1976 Yves St Laurent created his peasant look. This is a great summer alternative to the 50s sundress. Tiered skirts were combined with off-the-shoulder blouses inspired by the seventeenth century. Embroidered fabrics from Mexico and appliquéd cheesecloth (gauzelike cotton) were trend staples.

Making a 'Dorothy bag' was a popular way to round off an outfit. This small, pouchlike bag would match your frock, it either came ready-made or was included in the pattern if you were making your own (knitted or cloth).

The 70s cannot be discussed without mentioning disco. Studio 54 and *Saturday Night Fever* were responsible for a million dance floors bristling with static energy. The halterneck jumpsuit was a major player. Virtually backless, it was equally daringly low at the front.

Left and above: The influences of the 30s can be seen here in Hazel's A-line dress suit in the small raised shoulders, matching buttons and back belt details. The look is brought into the 70s with an oversized Biba silk blouse with balloon sleeves, maroon leather shoulder bag and 70s snakeskin wedges.

Top 70s tip
Buy a lovely wide-brim plain felt hat (as seen on page 81) in a green, dark pink, beige or black and accessorise with a long, thin scarf of your choice, tied around the brim to coordinate with your outfit.

Day Look

Bethan is channelling her inner Goldie Hawn wearing an ankle-length cotton maxi dress with cap sleeves and ric rac trim around the neckline. The look is finished off with sandal clogs, wooden jewellery and a semicircular wicker basket. The dress could be swapped for a kaftan for a more laid-back bohemian look.

Evening Look

Annie is working her photoshoot in a wide-legged halter-neck lycra jumpsuit with a matching tasselled scarf tied at the bodice. The oversized floral print is characteristic of the 70s. The look is finished with a wide brimmed nude felt hat and black platform shoes. For colder nights this would look great with a cropped faux-fur jacket.

The 1980s

"The higher up you go, the more mistakes you are allowed. Right at the top, if you make enough of them, it's considered to be your style." Fred Astaire

The 80s was a decade that took the best of past fashions and reinvented them in an exaggerated, almost cartoon-like manner. It scooped up every major trend and made it bigger, bolder (but, arguably, not better). The drop waist of the 1920s, the peplums of the 1940s and bold floral designs of the 50s were all reclaimed by the decade that fashion forgot. The firm rule for 1980s dressing is big is good, but bigger is better.

Day look shopping list

- Oversized polka dots
- Wide-brimmed hats
- Fingerless lace gloves
- Ra-ra skirts
- Puff-ball skirts
- Shoulder pads in knitwear and blouses
- Jodhpurs
- Stretchy jersey dresses
- Pastels, acids or neons
- Jelly shoes
- Pointy courts
- Collarless jackets
- Double-breasted blazers
- Batwing sleeves

Evening look shopping list

- Strapless prom dresses
- Giant puffed sleeves
- Sequinned jumpsuits
- Ball gowns
- High slits
- Metallic bows
- Chunky gold
- Chain belts
- Clutchbags
- Strong vibrant colours – fuschia, turquoise, bright peach, jade and red

Right: Harriet's wide-brimmed hat and fitted jacket with military-inspired frogging hark back to the style of the late 40s. The jersey material and oversized shoulder pads bring it back to the 80s.

Below: Astral motif detail on a cropped boxy jacket.

Opposite: Accessories were brash: bows, fruit, and studs were popular.

Main shapes, looks and influences

The 1980s saw a stratospheric rise in the number of trends and subcultures. A few are certainly worth a mention; the Club Kids, the New Romantics, the Johnny-come-lately punks left over from the late 70s. Films like *Flashdance* made leggings and cropped sweatshirts fashionable for the young. The MTV generation brought with it the fad for retina scarring neon. Whilst it is tempting to recreate these trends, the looks picked here, I believe, will become future classics for everyday dressing.

Power dressing, inspired by shows such as *Dynasty* and *Dallas*, encouraged the fashion excess that really made for a show-stopping 80s look. Think the biggest shoulder pads you can manage; and diamonds, pearls and gold (fake or real) in oversize shapes, for day and evening. A top-notch power dressing look can be finished off with barely black tights.

The big, and as of yet, unemulated icon of the 1980s was Princess Diana. Credited with reviving the trend for hats, she knew how to dress for the occasion – an art somewhat lost today. Low pumps, wrap dresses and a coy, demure look finished off with a wispy up-do and a large hat.

Clutch bags were popular – the larger, the better. Chanel's quilted chain strap bag was copied a million times over and is still a wardrobe staple today. Costume jewellery saw a huge resurgence in popularity. The chunky novelty items of the

1950s lost any remaining finesse and were left as hunks of gold plate or enamelled in garish primary colours. Astronomy influenced jewellery with stars, moon and planets colliding all over the same brooch or jacket. If it wasn't astral, it was covered in animals or bows.

One of my favourite looks was the matching bag and shoe combo. The 80s saw an increase in popularity of shoes that could be dyed to match your dress, bag, hat or all three at once. Brands such as Charles Jourdan and Roland Cartier created entire accessories ranges in rainbow-bright colours, ready to finish off any outfit.

Left: Hazel's harem trouser legs are an 80s update on the 70s jumpsuit.

Below: Power dressing in shiny leopard print. Note again the popularity of 40s detailing in the pleated hip detail.

Whilst disco disappeared in the early 80s, the block colours and sequins of this era clung on for a little while longer in evening wear. The jumpsuit also carried over, though with a tapered leg – as worn by Hazel (left) – and often incorporated a wide bat-winged top.

Daywear was loose and comfortable. If you were not wearing leggings and an oversized jumper, then you were pretty much guaranteed to be wearing a polycotton dress (minimal ironing required) with an elasticated waist. These dresses copied the styles of the late 1940s and early 1950s. Peplums came back in – as seen on this gold dress (left) and red jacket (page 84). Pretty, full-skirted floral dresses, with nipped-in waists sold in abundance from Laura Ashley.

Top 80s tip

How do you differentiate a 50s dress from an 80s dress? This is a serious problem amongst vintage sellers because many are still passing off 80s clothing as earlier, whether knowingly or not. 80s dresses were mass-produced and exaggerated. There just isn't the same attention to detail. Note the lack of darting around the bodice and the absence of the shelf bust. There is a big difference in sleeves. An 80s dress has sleeves a few inches above the elbow, generally straight up and down, compared to the neat cap-sleeve of the 1950s. Take a look at the waist. Is there elastic hidden under that matching fabric belt? If so, I would happily put a punt on it being 80s and not 50s. Also, does that drop-V waist have a piped edging? Run a mile.

Above: Diana epitomised the 80s trend for matching accessories and ladylike outfits.

Day Look

Harriet wears a classic 80s wrap dress by Cockney Rebel, with oversized buttons and polka dots. Note the tulip shape of the skirt exposing the knee. Her white leather shoulder bag and matching court shoe both feature popular gold chain-link detailing. Oversized pearl clip-on earrings complete her look.

Evening Look

Hazel is wearing a full-length white evening dress with side split, plunging V-neck and long sleeves. This look references late 70s disco and is brought back into the 80s by the the sequins and shoulder pads. Plenty of gold jewellery and a matching clutch bag and stiletto sandal turn this in an evening look that could easily be worn today.

Useful Extras

Underwear and shapewear

Having the right underwear can make a huge difference to how clothes sit on you. Don't be afraid, the era of rib-crunching discomfort is long gone. Many fans of vintage and good faux vintage lingerie enjoy the ceremony that comes with attaching your stockings and tweaking your foundation garments, and once you get used to it, it no longer seems quite so tortuous.

A great tragedy about women today is that so many seem to have given up on their waists, or forgotten that they have one at all! The catwalks of the Noughties have given us a trend for hipster jeans and low-slung skirts. Combine this with a fear of a 'muffin top' and we get a too-heavy reliance on baggy clothing. Let us not surrender the natural hourglass curves that make us beautiful – and this is just the shape that vintage fashions highlight so wonderfully! Most girls I know who regularly wear vintage have managed to train their muscles to attain the 'vintage shape' without any recourse to the gym, so let's relocate that fabulous space between our lowest ribs and our hip-bones and put some beautiful curves back on the streets.

Featured here we have two different ways of neatening the waist : the 7" Baby Corset, the one to wear under New Look dresses (opposite); and the Corselette (page 96), introduced in the late 1950s and still worn today. Both are clever reproductions from What Katie Did.

A brief history of underwear

In the 1920s, bras were little more than camisoles, though if you were blessed with larger assets the Symington Side Lacer was a contraption designed to lace up at the sides, enabling ladies to flatten their busts in line with the fashions of the day. This was a big change from the fashions of the previous decade, which pretty much dictated that a woman should squeeze herself into a lace-up corset, boned to draconian proportions. The corset lingered from the 20s to the 50s, but not everyone chose to wear one. The 1930s saw the arrival of the bra almost as we know it, with adjustable back sizes and cup sizes. The construction was not as refined, though, and it was generally made up of three pieces of fabric sewn into a cone.

Contrary to popular belief, the controversial Sweater Girl look first appeared in the 30s. In fact, it was thanks to Lana Turner's appearance in the 1937 film *They Won't Forget*, all pointy boobs and tight cashmere sweater, that the stitched bullet bra enjoyed so much success in the 1950s.

You can forget about the racy colours associated with modern garments. Until the 60s they were functional affairs in a white or peach satin or cotton. Underwiring gave everyone a boost in the 1950s, whilst post-1960 a rounded cup, more commonly associated with current brassières, became de rigueur. In terms of undies, the Tap Pant, as seen on page 95 in black, was popular till the 40s, after which the elasticated baby doll brief was introduced and is still the preferred pant of choice for many women today. Raciness returned in the 1980s with teddies, lace all-in-ones and French knickers.

Left: Bra Strap holders (also known as 'lingerie guards'), a packet of 60s stockings and 60s suspender belt.

Swimwear

Up until the 1930s bathing suits were generally made out of wool. Ladies' swimsuits comprised what we would consider today to be quite a full covering: a skirt, blouse and even stockings. Annette Kellerman, an Australian professional swimmer and film star, stirred things up in 1907 when she bathed publicly in a 'body stocking' and was promptly arrested for indecency.

The 20s swimsuit still covered the majority of the body, although they tended to be a less complex 'one-piece'.

The 'two-piece' swimsuit first made its appearance in the 30s. At the same time one-pieces and play suits became form-fitting.

In 1946 the 'two-piece' became known as the 'bikini'. It was first introduced by French fashion designer Louis Reard and was named after Bikini Atoll, a nuclear bomb testing site.

50s swimsuits (as pictured here, including one for an infant) were cotton affairs that were not terribly practical for the beach, but embodied the colourful prints and designs of the decade.

By the 1960s swimwear was the more practical garment we use today. It was actually designed with the water in mind!

In the 70s Farah Fawcett single-handedly brought back the craze for the one piece swimsuit or 'maillot'. This time it was high-legged, sexy and tight. This trend lasted well into the 80s.

How to get into vintage clothes

In this section I tell you, literally, how to get into vintage clothes. Over the years I have seen many a frustrated person getting stuck in a frock, only to promptly discard it out of sheer annoyance. With a little bit of careful planning, that same dress would have slipped on easily and fitted a treat. Paying attention to this section will make friends of your local shopkeepers, as a little care results in far less damage to the clothing. (I speak as someone who has had to cut herself out of two dresses because of the zips.)

- Firstly, have a good hard look at the garment. Where does it open?

- Is the belt undone? These are quite often tied onto the garments via the belt loops or even sleeves. Also check for ties and ribbons.

- Check the sides for shorter zips and the back for longer zips. It's not that unusual for a dress to have both.

- Check that the poppers or buttons commonly used to taper long sleeves have been undone.

- Check for built-in slips or corsetry that may bunch up as you put it on.

- Once you are sure everything has been undone, proceed as follows:

- Zips down the back – step into it.

- Zips at the side (common in pre-50s clothes) – put it on over your head.

- If you need to put it over your head, the Number One tip is this: put your hands through the armholes first, then pull over by your head and shoulders, not the other way around. This is the golden rule for not getting stuck in a dress. Most vintage clothing has very little stretch, and 99% of the time you will get your head in and find that you have no room to manoeuvre your arms and shoulders.

- If it doesn't go over your shoulders, don't force it; it certainly will not go over your hips.

- Once in, make sure you have done everything up again, take stock of how it feels and looks (in a full-length mirror) and then make your decision.

How to repair and maintain vintage

Now that you are building yourself your own treasure trove, make you sure you treat it with the same level of care that has allowed it to last this long.

Repairs

Some repairs are easy to do yourself. Others such as replacing zips are better left to the professionals. That said, an old padded sewing box filled with interesting bits and bobs and a pile of items to rescue can make for a very relaxing afternoon.

Avoid where possible cutting hem lines. Instead, fold the fabric no more than twice to the desired length and press well with an iron (on the inside). Then lightly hand-stitch with transparent nylon thread, which is available from all good haberdashers.

If you really must shorten a dress or skirt, keep the spare fabric, don't throw it away. It can be used for making a tie belt if the original is missing or a matching head scarf. Even the smallest scrap can be handy for a repair.

If you come across unpatterned cheap silk scarves, snap them up and keep them for the sewing box. When repairing a tear or moth hole, use a small square of silk to back fabric when darning. The lightweight nature of silk makes it easy to sew through both layers and adds extra reinforcement. This works especially well if you are trying to rescue damaged underarms.

So, what is darning? Well, it's an old-fashioned technique to repair damaged fabric in an area that is away from a seam. Make small neat stitches in silk or wool thread (not cotton) over and around the damaged area, where possible in the same direction of the weave or grain. This can also be applied to patterned fabric so long as you carefully match the threads to the colours.

Once old and much-loved clothes become
beyond repair and destined for the rag pile,
remove the buttons and keep for a new creation
or to add to an existing garment that may
need sprucing up.

Washing

The first time you wash a newly acquired vintage treasure can be fairly nerve-wracking, so proceed with caution.

Start off by soaking it in cold water to lift any surface dirt, then gently run the warm tap to see if the colour starts to run. If the sink starts to fill with darks hues of dye, take the garment out and start again on a cooler temperature. This is a common occurrence in crêpe fabric.

If you do feel safe to proceed with the washing machine, always set it to a short run with minimal spin at 30°C. Wash delicate fabrics in a closed cotton pillowcase to stop them being pulled around in the drum. This also works a treat for hosiery and underwear.

Don't machine-wash sequins or glass beads. Even modern ones will melt or discolour. I would also avoid ever machine-washing silk (which goes crispy) or crêpe (which shrinks).

Top tip
For wiffy garments you cannot wash at all, use cheap undiluted vodka in a spritzer bottle and spray the armpits. Works a treat! Removes smells better than dry cleaning.

Stains

- Candlewax – place a piece of brown paper over the wax area. Iron over the paper with a warm iron. Wax melts and gets sealed into the paper! Genius!

- Lipstick – with a knife, scrape away as much lipstick as possible. Apply some washing-up liquid and rub into the stain, then gently dab with water to remove the stain. Repeat if needed.

- Chewing gum – place the item in a plastic bag. Pop the bagged item into freezer. Leave overnight. Remove the item from the bag, and the gum can be scraped clean off!

Drying and pressing

Cotton and linen dries effortlessly and can be ironed without much fear. With anything, start on a very low iron temperature so as not to melt the surface. Certain old synthetic fabrics, including some types of crêpe, will go shiny when heated. Equally, satins may go matte. If in doubt, iron inside out. If you have a serious vintage collection, invest in a home steamer.

If you are hanging washing out on the line, fold the garment at the waist to avoid the damp weight hanging from the shoulders. If it's sunny, cover with an old bit of sheet to avoid bleaching.

Storage

Store everything clean, as moths love dirt. If you can't afford garment bags, place any items for storage in a clean receptacle, high enough to avoid being nibbled by mice.

Avoid hanging garments on metal hangers, as the thinness of the metal can ruin the shape of the shoulder. Invest in padded or wooden hangers. Don't leave your vintage on a rail or cupboard exposed to sunlight, or you will find that the exposed side will fade.

Wrap delicates in pH neutral tissue paper. Most standard paper is acidic and potentially harmful to silk or wool objects.

Labels to look out for

A little label savviness can help you spot fakes and also date garments. If you see an interesting label, a quick internet search can yield wonders. My favourite resource for checking labels is the Vintage Fashion Guild Website. This guide illustrates the changes in fashion labels from the elegant flourish of the 50s and before, to the typography seen today.

Here is a non-exhaustive list of designers, fashion houses and brands you may not know:

- Radley
- Blanes
- Suzy Perrette
- Bill Gibb
- Granny takes a trip
- Alice Pollock

- Clare McCardell
- Janice Wrainright
- Thea Porter
- Swirl
- Droopy and Brown
- Hattie Carnegie

- John Bates for Jean Varon
- Emma Domb
- Ceil Chapman
- Frank Usher
- Jacques Heim
- Lilli Ann
- Alice Edwards
- Susan Small
- Sambo Fashions
- Marshall & Snelgrove

Top tip

Look out for old Laura Ashley labels without the blue circle on them. These 70s dresses are highly sought-after.

Where to shop

Once you start to look for vintage, you see it everywhere. In the meantime, here are some recommended hunting grounds. You may find if you are a novice that you come home empty-handed from your first few outings. Don't worry, though; it's better to avoid so-so items than to purchase and regret.

- Charity shops – my tip is to go to hospice shops, which often have entire wardrobes donated.

- Vintage shops – these can be expensive, but a good one will be honestly priced. Larger shops may also have too much stock, so if you don't mind rummaging you may find a mislabelled and underpriced item.

- Carboot fares – be prepared to rummage. This is where a good knowledge of print is helpful, as you may catch only a glimpse of fabric peeking out from under a pile of junk.

- Dress agencies – they are very fussy, so good for iconic pieces that will be classics 20 years down the line. Clean and in the best condition, but expect to pay a designer price.

- Auctions – look out for job lots. One good item can redeem an entire lot. Get rid of any undesirables by hosting a 'swishing' or vintage swap shop party.

- If you are a serious collector, put an ad in the paper or online and wait for a house clearance to come up. Quite often, people have no idea what to do with old clothing.

- On the Net – online shopping has become very popular, although eBay is not what it used to be. Etsy does yield interesting items, but I prefer online boutiques. See my list of carefully curated retailers on page 109 for vintage sellers you can trust.

Recommended reading

www.retrochick.co.uk Vintage fashion blogger, whisky drinker, social media flutterby. Blogging about vintage events in pretty frocks, and whatever else she fancies. The authority on Vanity Sizing.

www.pennydreadfulvintage.com Margaret blogs about vintage fashion, and also has a penchant for books, history, London, and sweet things. Check out her shop as well.

www.theatreoffashion.co.uk Authored by a costume historian who doubles as a trend forecaster, this website traces current trends back to their historical precedents, with an emphasis on all that is theatrical in fashion.

www.vintagebrighton.com Celebrates the South Coast's thriving vintage scene.

www.clothesonfilm.com The best website I have found for cinematic referencing.

www.redlegsinsoho.blogspot.com Min writes the most eloquent blog charting her London-based adventures.

www.brightyoungtwins.blogspot.com Two best friends blogging about their time warped existence.

www.landgirl1980.blogspot.com Charly has a penchant for women's history, headscarves and vintage-inspired frockery.

www.rockalily.com Ree Ree blogs about her rockabilly and vintage-themed life.

www.thevintagetraveler.wordpress.com Always ready for a roadtrip, especially in search of vintage treasures or fashion history.

www.jointhestylehighclub.com Lena's personal style blog features vintage news, shopping tips and unusual style muses.

www.theglamourologist.blogspot.com Lucy blogs about the intriguing history of cosmetics, make up & style. One lipstick at a time.

www.perditaspursuits.blogspot.com Perdita's Pursuits is all about having a fabulous time on a modest income, combining thrift, vintage and a little bit of the unusual.

www.straighttalkingmama.blogspot.com A vintage-loving 40-something talking about her life-long love of vintage clothes, homewares, in fact just about everything.

www.thevintageguidetolondon.com The ultimate guide to all things vintage in London.

www.vintagefashionguild.org Home to the best label directory I have seen.

Online vintage shops

www.junosayshello.com Juno Says Hello is a London-based online boutique selling luxury vintage dresses.

www.lovelysvintageemporium.com This is a trend-led vintage fashion and accessories website owned by a magazine fashion stylist and editor.

www.natashabailie.com Natasha sells the best 50s dresses on the net. Also has her own range of 50s-style repro.

www.lovemissdaisy.com Mother and daughter-run boutique full of beautiful cherry-picked pieces from around the world. Stockist of vintage wedding dresses.

www.corinacorina.com Well priced vintage and reworked clothing.

Introduction

Have you ever wanted to primp and coiffure your hair to perfection? Or been inspired by the golden ages of fashion and silver screen goddesses? Hairstyles throughout the decades have been the foundation of many a vintage look, but the techniques used to create them, once taken for granted, are now fading from modern girls' repertoires.

In this book you will find step-by-step techniques for achieving perfect pompadours, outrageous beehives and other essential styles to help transform yourself into a vintage vixen. I've included some of the most iconic hairstyles that made their mark over the decades to become the most inspiring and influential looks of the last century.

Remember though, be patient! Some of these styles take a bit of practise to master. Even the most skilled of hairstylists don't always get it right first time!

EXPERIMENT

Each technique given is just a guide. There are many different ways to personalise your vintage 'do'. Try rolling your barrel curls or pin curls in a different direction, for instance. You may find something that really works for you.

THE HAIRCUT

Your haircut is important. The cut that makes it easiest to create a vintage look is a simple one-length style, perhaps with a few soft layers through the bottom of your hair. That's not to say that more modern and heavily layered hairstyles cannot be transformed into an immaculately coiffed victory roll or a perfect peek-a-boo. It's just a little easier with a classic cut.

Some of the retro styles suit a fringe, others work better without. You have to decide what works best for you in terms of having a fringe cut or not.

Good luck and have fun!

Belinda

Essential Equipment

There are a number of 'essential' items you will need to help you create your vintage look, which I have listed over the following pages. You can mostly find these at hairdressing suppliers, department stores and chemists. However, you won't necessarily need all of these items at once. With time and experience you can usually modify techniques to suit your hairdressing style and the available equipment.

Sectioning clips, combs and brushes are definitely essential for creating most styles. To help you further, at the beginning of each style in this book, I have included a list of the equipment that you will need.

Decorative items are always lovely to add to your finished your style. Try fresh or silk flowers, a string of pearls or pretty hair clips, depending on what look you are after. Scarves and ribbons can also be used to give your style an extra special retro touch. See pages 100–107 for tips on styling retro scarves. Don't forget that hats were often an essential part of vintage outfits. Try adding a little pillbox hat to your bouffant to complete your look.

Hairdryer or portable hood dryer

Nowadays you can buy small portable hood dryers that have small motors attached to them. Or, sometimes, you may find they have an attachment for your hairdryer.

Curling tongs

You can buy these in different sizes, but if you can only have one, buy a medium-sized tong, around 30 mm diameter.

Pin-curl clips
(pictured left)

These little silver two-pronged clips are used to hold your pin curls in place.

Kirby grips

You can buy Kirby grips in different sizes and colours. Find them to match your hair colour so it's easier to disguise them and they blend into your hairstyle.

Hair padding

Used to create extra volume, especially in beehives. I have included a guide to making one of your own on page 108.

Boar bristle brush
Made from natural fibres, this brush is the best one to use for smoothing out your hairstyle.

Sectioning clips
Sectioning clips are essential for creating your hairstyle. They will help you to keep your hair tucked firmly out of the way when you are dealing with different sections of your hair.

Backcombing brush
This is a brush of a similar shape to a pintail comb, except it has bristles instead of teeth. You can use this to backcomb or to smooth out your shape.

Pintail comb
This is a comb with a thin, pointy metal or plastic end. It is perfect to use to divide your hair sections cleanly or to backcomb.

Regular comb
This is the best comb to gently comb out knots and tangles after you have shampooed and conditioned your hair.

Rollers (various sizes)
You can use these to 'wet-set' your hair, or roll up sections as you are blow drying to create extra volume. Velcro rollers are the most readily available. You need to buy these in a size that will allow your hair to be wrapped around the roller two and a half to three times.

Heated rollers
These are usually sold in packs of set sizes in department stores and hairdressing suppliers.

Hairspray
You will need plenty of this. Hairspray is essential to keep your hairstyle rock solid. It will also help to give your style volume and support.

Synthetic hair pieces
You can find these, readymade, in different sizes and shapes. The most common is a doughnut shape. You can cut them down to the size you require.

Hairnet
Hairnets are great for protecting your hair overnight – to stop you getting 'bed head'; or you can use them to creating padding for your style.

The Styles

Finger Waves & Pin Curls

During the flapper era, fashions were boyish. Women's figures were hidden beneath straight-cut dresses, hemlines became shorter and so did hair lengths. Cropped bobs became very popular in the 1920s, but were first seen in Hollywood on the American actress Irene Castle, who had worn her hair in this way as early as 1914. Finger waves were often used to soften the masculine edge of a bob.

The difference between a finger wave and a Marcel wave is that finger waves, also known as water waves, are created on wet hair, whereas a Marcel wave is created by using heat on dry hair. Finger waves were often seen alongside pin curls, which were almost always used to style and finish the ends of the hair. In old-fashioned hairdressing, the general rule was to have 3 waves and 2 rows of pin curls.

You will need
Styling products, such as gel, mousse or setting lotion
Barbering comb
Pin-curl clips
Water spray bottle
A portable dryer
(you can buy these from hairdressing suppliers and some department stores)
Boar bristle brush

Step 1
Shampoo and towel dry your hair.

Step 2
Apply a generous amount of setting lotion, mousse or gel. Your hair needs to remain completely saturated throughout the styling process for the fingerwaves to be successful.

Step 3
Part your hair on your preferred side and comb it through, distributing the hair evenly and in a natural fall around your head (Fig.1). It is important for the hair to be distributed evenly so that there is enough hair for each row of finger waves.

Step 4
Comb your hair back away from your hair line (Fig. 2). You are going to create a 'c' shape. Place your middle finger flat along your scalp where you wish to make your first wave. Apply pressure with your middle finger so you don't disturb the hair you have already combed back to start your 'c' and comb the hair smoothly in a downwards motion.

Step 5

Once the hair is combed through smoothly, keeping your middle finger in place, comb the hair forwards (Fig.3). At this stage your comb should be in an upright position.

Step 6

Once you have begun to comb the hair forward in a 'c' shape, you need to flatten the comb to your scalp and push up towards your middle finger. Once you reach the middle finger with your comb, lift the comb back to an upright position (Fig. 4). This will create the crest of the wave. Keeping your middle finger fixed on your scalp, place your index finger on the other side of the upright comb. Now you have your middle and index fingers both applying pressure on the scalp – one finger on either side of the comb.

Step 7

With your pin-curl clips, pin either side of the crest lifting your fingers up slightly so the grips can slide into place (Fig.5).

Step 8

It is very important to make sure your hair has been combed in a natural fall so you don't have gaps in your crests and waves. Make a second crest and wave behind the first one using the same techniques from steps 4 to 7. You need to place your middle finger in line with the first placing so that you can make the crests join together in the second wave (Fig.6).

Step 9

Form the second crest as before in line with the first, and place clips either side (Figs. 7 and 8).

Step 10

Continue this all the way around the head through the crown until you reach the other hairline.

Step 11

Start the second row of waves from the opposite hairline using the same technique (steps 4 to 10), although this time you will be creating a 'backwards c' (Fig. 9). Continue this all the way around the head again to the opposite hairline. You need to continue to make runs of curls until you get to the occipital bone, where your head dips in to the nape of your neck.

Pin curls
(*steps 12 to 15*)
You can use this technique with finger waves or on its own, pin-curling your entire head of hair. Pin curls are a fundamental part of vintage hairstyling and the essence of this technique is adapted and used in different forms throughout this book.

Step 12

Now you have some lengths of hair that are loose at the end of your fingerwaves. Take up a row of hair at the bottom of the fingerwaves about 2 cm wide. You are going to split this into sections about 2 cm thick. This can be done as you go along, creating a small, square base for your pin curl to sit on.

Step 13

Each row of pin curls should be curled in the same direction. Let's call them 'b'-shaped and 'd'-shaped.

Look at the direction of your last wave – 'c' or 'backwards c'. This will determine which way your pin curl will be placed as you need to continue creating a flowing waveform.

If your last fingerwave was a 'c' shape, your next pin curl will be a 'd' shape. Likewise, a 'backwards c' should follow with a 'b' shape pin curl.

You need to take the hair from your small square section and, holding the very tips of your hair between your forefinger and thumb, and alternating your left and right hand, begin to roll up the curl towards the base of the section (Fig. 10). Always hold the ends of your hair in the curl with thumb and forefinger. You will see how the pin curl will look like a 'b' or 'd' shape.

Step 14

Once you have rolled up your pin curl , use a pin-curl clip to secure the curl in place. The clip needs to be placed into the curl at and through the base, so it is holding the curl firmly (Fig. 11).

Step 15

Finish the row of pin curls and start the next row, but this time you need to curl your pin curls in the opposite direction to the last row. This will continue the wave through to the end (Figs. 12 and 13).

Step 16

Dry your hair (Fig. 14).

You can let your hair dry naturally, although this could take some time depending on the thickness of your hair – up to 12 hours. Alternatively, you can sit under a portable soft dryer. You can find these at department stores and hairdressing suppliers. Under a dryer the process could take up to 45 minutes, depending on your hair thickness.

*It is very important to make sure your finger waves are bone dry. If there is a hint of moisture in your hair when you come to brush them out, you will lose the wave.

Step 17

Once your hair is completely dry, remove all of the clips from your hair and start to brush out. You need to start from the bottom, using your fingers to push the waves back into place.

You could also leave your hair untouched if you would like a sleek, wet look (Fig. 15).

Step 18

Spray with hairspray to hold.

The Peek-a-boo

Made famous by Veronica Lake, the peek-a-boo has been imitated and adapted by many of today's fashion icons. Considered one of the most seductive hairstyles, we see, again and again, modern sirens such as Dita Von Teese, Scarlett Johansson, Kim Basinger and Evan Rachel Wood pay tribute to this hairstyle's ability to transform them instantly into a silver-screen goddess…

A peek-a-boo is usually styled on hair that is shoulder length or longer.

You will need
Hairdryer
Round brushes
Curling tongs
Pin-curl clips
Hairspray
Comb
Soft bristle brush for smoothing

Step 1

Wash your hair and then blow dry your hair with volume. To increase volume, you can put rollers in your hair and blow dry, use heated rollers, or blow dry and pin your hair in rolls using pin-curl clips.

Step 2

Once your hair is blow-dried and curled up in the rollers or clips, spray with hairspray and leave for 10–15 minutes for it to cool down.

Step 3

Remove all of the rollers/clips and part your hair on the side. Choose the side that will give your hair the greatest volume for the wave at the top. Give it all another light hairspray.

Step 4

Brush out all of the curl with a soft padded brush (if you have hair that doesn't hold a curl well, it's best to miss out this step).

Step 5

Part your hair, taking your sections vertically and roughly 4 cm back from your front hairline.

Step 6

Take a small rectangular section on the heavy side of your parting, about 2 cm thick, and put your curling tongs in at the root (Fig. 1).

*Be careful not to burn yourself. Try resting a comb between the hot tongs and your scalp, so the tongs don't come into contact with your scalp.

Holding the mid-lengths of the section between your thumb and forefinger, wind and twist the section around the tong until you get to the end of your hair. The twist is very important.

*Try not to wind the section too tightly, you still want to be able to roll the tongs while you are waiting for the curl to set. You also need to be able to slide the tong out from your curl when it has been heated enough.

Let the spring flap close over the tip of the curl and hold the tong until the hair has sufficiently heated. This should take about 15-20 seconds.

Step 7
Release the ends from the tong and slide your hair section out over the tongs without disturbing the curl. Clip the curled section with a pin-curl clip again and leave to cool.

Step 8
Repeat this process with the whole front hairline. If you wish, you can do this over the whole of your head, but it's not necessary.

Step 9
Take out all of the clips and brush the waves into shape (Fig. 2), adjusting the top wave to get the perfect peek-a-boo shape and brushing the ends under and towards your face.

Step 10
Give it all a healthy coating of hairspray to hold.

Victory Rolls

The iconic 1940s wartime hairstyle.

In the early 1940s, during World War II, women were rolling up their sleeves and getting involved in the war effort. Fashion was changing due to shortages of fabric and the need to ration. Hairstyles also needed to be practical, as women were being employed to work in factories while their husbands went off to war.

Supposedly named after the manoeuvres of fighter planes, victory rolls were a great way to arrange hair, keeping it safely away from machinery and leaving room to put on a hat without quashing the style!

Modelled at one point by Veronica Lake in a short film encouraging ladies to style their hair in this way, it has become one of our favourite hairstyles to reproduce for a forties revival look.

You will need
Heated rollers *or* hairdryer and pin-curl clips
Combs for backcombing and sectioning
Boar bristle brush for smoothing
Kirby grips
Hairspray

Step 1

Prepare your hair, creating volume using heated rollers or blow drying with a round brush and securing sections with pin-curl clips. Once set, remove your rollers/clips and part your hair on the preferred side.

Step 2

Section and secure your hair into four (Fig.1).

Section 1: your fringe. Take a triangle section from mid-way back on the top of your head to just above both of your temples.

Section 2: left side. Section the whole front part of your hair from the top of your head to the top of your ear.

Section 3: right side, as above.

*One of the sections will probably have more hair in it, because of your side parting.

Section 4: the back of your hair.

Step 3

Backcomb the first side section of your hair for volume and padding. Backcomb taking smaller vertical sections, about 1–2 cm through the larger section (Fig. 2).

Step 4

Roll your hair loosely over your hand, rather like rolling a French pleat. You should be able to hold the finished

roll securely with one finger so you can see the shape of your victory roll. When you are happy with how it looks, pin it into place and spray with hairspray (Fig. 3). Repeat steps 3 and 4 with the other side section.

Step 5
Backcomb your fringe (Fig. 4). Smooth out the top layer of the backcombing ready to roll it into the rest of the victory rolls.

Step 6
Roll your fringe loosely around your middle three fingers, away from your parting. Try to get the roll the same size as the largest of your two victory rolls. Pin this into place so that the second roll meets up with your fringe roll (Fig. 5). Now it looks like one roll.

Step 7
Backcomb the back section of your hair for a little extra shape and volume. Smooth over the top layers with your boar bristle brush (Fig. 6).

The beauty of this style is that victory rolls can be created on hair that is bobbed, very long and every length in between.

135

Step 8

Using Kirby grips, start fixing a row of support grips along your nape (Fig. 7), about 2 cm above your hairline. Each grip should cross over for extra support.

Step 9

Once this has been securely clipped, section the ends of your hair into three parts: the centre and two sides.

Step 10

Backcomb each section very lightly if you need to, smoothing out the underneath layers, as this is the part you will see. Reverse roll each section over your hand and clip into place (Fig. 8).

Your rolls need to be roughly the same size so you can make each section blend together to make one large reverse roll along your back hairline.

Step 11

Spray hair well to smooth down any stray hairs and you have your finished look.

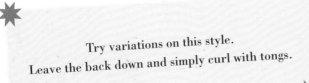

Try variations on this style.
Leave the back down and simply curl with tongs.

The Poodle

A popular hairstyle of the forties and fifties, made famous by Lucille Ball and also Betty Grable's iconic 1943 pin-up picture.

In the fifties, curls and soft hairstyles were in! It was considered sophisticated to have curly hair. Fortunately perms had become safer and the results more reliable. So if you were unlucky enough to be a straight-haired girl at this time, you would be off to the hairdresser every six weeks to have a perm. You could even buy a permanent wave kit and try your hand at home. This was an essential part of the hair-care regime for any woman wishing to emulate the poodle and many other styles of the forties and fifties.

This is an interpretation of the fifties Poodle.

You will need
Curling tongs
Hairdryer
Heated rollers, rollers or pin-curl clips
Round brush
Pin-curl clips
Kirby grips and fringe pins
Hairspray

Step 1

Prep your hair to create maximum volume using heated rollers or curling tongs (Figs. 1 and 2). Alternatively, blow dry and secure the hair into curls with pin-curl clips.

Step 2

Spray well with hairspray and leave to cool down for 5–10 minutes.

Step 3

Remove all of your rollers/clips and section your hair into 2 parts (Fig. 3).

Section 1: take a horseshoe-shape section through the top of your head. *This is a curved section from your temple through your crown to your other temple.

Section 2: the rest of your hair (the bottom half). This will be split into 3 later.

Clip the bottom section out of the way.

Step 4

If your hair is still quite straight, use curling tongs to create more curls in the top horseshoe section (Fig. 4).

Step 5

Using Kirby grips, start to loosely pin the top into place, making voluminous curls within the section (Fig. 5). Fix these into place with hairspray.

Step 6

Split and clip the bottom section into 3 sections (Fig. 6).
    1: Left side. 2: Right side. 3: Back of your head.

Step 7

Backcomb the sides gently and twist them up to meet the curls in the top section. Secure with grips and leave the ends out to style later (Fig. 7).

Step 8
Take the back section up to meet the top curly section and, as for the sides, secure with grips (Fig. 8). Again, leave the ends out to curl and secure later.

Step 9
With your curling tongs, curl all of the remaining loose ends (Fig. 9).

Step 10
Arrange all the curls into shape, secure with grips (Fig. 10) and give a final spray with hairspray to hold.

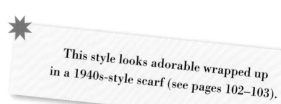

This style looks adorable wrapped up in a 1940s-style scarf (see pages 102–103).

The VV Forward Fringe Roll

This style is ideal for anyone who doesn't have a fringe.

The fringe roll is an adaptation of the Bettie Page fringe. Bettie Page was the notorious pin-up girl made famous in the fifties by posing for Hugh Hefner. Never quite as mainstream as Marilyn, she nevertheless developed a cult following and later in life was even the subject of a motion picture. The rolled fringe was fashioned by girls so they could emulate Bettie's trademark fringe without having to commit to a full fringe cut.

The rolled fringe can also be used in conjunction with victory rolls.

You will need
Kirby grips
Hair padding (roly poly)
Hair ties
Curling tongs
Combs
Hairspray

Step 1

Take a small triangle section at the front of your head from the recessions of your front hairline (this is usually where your hairline starts to curve around towards your temples). Secure it out of the way (Fig. 1).

Step 2

Secure the rest of your hair into a ponytail (Fig. 2).

It looks super cute, if you have straight hair, to curl your ponytail using curling tongs.

Step 3

Removing the clip from your front section, take small sections and backcomb to give height and body. This will also make your hairstyle more stable.

Step 4

Smooth out your backcombing and take a small roly poly hair pad (you can find these in chemists or hairdressing suppliers). It needs to be the shape of a sausage or banana.

Roll the ends of your fringe over and around the hair pad, keeping tension from the roots of your hair as you go (Fig. 3).

Step 5

Secure the roll with grips on either side of your head and spread your hair around the padding to hide it (Fig. 4).

Step 6

Spray with hairspray to hold.

4

The final look

It is also possible to create this style without using a support piece. You just need to backcomb the whole fringe section, smooth out and roll under with your hands. Secure it by making sure your Kirby grips are fastened firmly underneath, to the hair at the front hairline.

The Marilyn Set

Women in the forties and fifties would spend hours styling their hair. It was usual to make regular weekly trips to the hairdresser for a shampoo and set. During the war, when money was tight, the weekly trips may have become fortnightly trips – this is when tying scarves came in very handy. Women would also have their own set of rollers and learned to roll up and pin curl their own hair at home. It wasn't unusual for women to spend all day working around the house with rollers in, setting their hair ready for their evening out.

You will need
Rollers and pins
Pin-tail comb
Portable dryer
Styling products

149

Step 1

Shampoo and towel dry your hair. Apply mousse, setting lotion or other styling products and comb though (Fig. 1).

Step 2

Section your hair into 5 (Fig. 2).

Section 1: a section, the width of your roller, directly over the centre of your head – from your front hairline to back hairline.

Section 2: a roller width down and through the front left side of your head.

Section 3: a roller width down and through the back left side of your head.

Section 4: a roller width down and through the front right side of your head.

Section 5: a roller width down and through the back right side of your head.

Secure all the sections out of the way.

Step 3

Start working on the first section of hair – the section that runs over the centre of your head.

Take a 2 cm section of hair horizontally across the front of the section. Comb this section straight up from your head. Hold the ends of the section between your thumb and index finger.

With the other hand place a roller at the end of your section and flip the ends of the hair over the top of the roller (Fig. 3).

Roll this up, use the end of a pintail comb to drag the ends under to the centre of the roller, so you don't get fishhooks (pieces of hair that are folded sharply in the wrong direction), as they make the ends of your hair look fluffy. Fix in place (Fig. 4).

Step 4
Continue this all the way through the centre section. You may need someone to help you with the back.

Step 5
Start rolling up the sides in the same way (Fig. 5). Each of the sections needs to be combed directly out from your head so the rollers are rolled on the base of your hair (the hair is directed straight out from the head once the roller is secure).

Step 6
Continue this for the entire head (see Figs. 6 and 7 for ideal placement of rollers).

Step 7

Once your hair has been completely rolled up into the set, you can either sit under a portable dryer (which should take about 30 minutes) or leave it to dry naturally (which could take 8–12 hours depending on the thickness of your hair).

Step 8

Remove all of the rollers once your hair is completely dry (Fig. 8).

Step 9

Using a boar bristle brush, start to brush out your curls (Fig. 9). You can be quite firm while brushing them out. Work the ends under with the brush and turn them inwards towards your face.

Step 10

Spray with hairspray to hold.

The Pompadour (Quiff)

This is a straightforward way to achieve a classic and fun fifties look.

The quiff or pompadour was a popular style in the fifties among the rockabilly guys. It was made famous by James Dean and years later by John Travolta in *Grease*, but was actually named after Madam de Pompadour, the chief mistress of King Louis XV of France.

This style has become a favourite with today's rockabilly girls because of its obvious nod to the fifties and the fact that it can usually be worn with a ponytail, which is great to swing and flip around while dancing!

Remember – there are many ways to style a pompadour. You can roll it different ways or wear it scruffy, depending on the length or your hair.

Alas! If you have a short fringe, you may have to grow it a bit to be able to quiff it. For this style you need to have a reasonably long fringe or no fringe at all.

You will need
Kirby grips
Comb
Hairspray
Ponytail elastic
Curling tongs

Step 1

Take a small triangle section at the front of your head from the recessions of your front hairline (this is usually where your hairline starts to curve around towards your temples). Secure it out of the way.

Step 2

Secure the rest of your hair into a ponytail.

It looks super cute, if you have straight hair, to curl your ponytail using curling tongs.

Step 3

Remove the clip from your front section. Take small sections and backcomb to give height and body. This will also make your hairstyle more stable.

Step 4

Smooth the front of the section out with a boar bristle brush and start to roll your hair around your 3 middle fingers. If you want a larger or smaller quiff use more or less fingers to roll your hair (Fig. 1).

*If you want a more modern quiff, you don't need to smooth out the backcombing.

Step 5

Use your finger as a makeshift Kirby grip before you secure the grip directly under your finger (Fig. 2). You may need to use a few grips to make sure it stays in place.

Step 6

Spray well with hairspray to hold.

This style looks great with a fifties-style scarf tied around the ponytail (see pages 106–107).

Work to Step 4, but instead of rolling backwards, try rolling to the side. Create a small barrel curl, so you can see through the centre of the roll from front on and secure as directed.

1

2

The Joan Beehive

The beehive was the most sought-after and replicated hairstyle of the 1960s and is still iconic of that time, along with the Beatles and the mini skirt. Given its name because of its similarity to the shape of old-fashioned beehives, it remains a popular hairstyle for weddings and social events, on the catwalk, and even as an every-day style for some.

In this book we have included two different styles of beehive, because there are so many different ways you can create this look. The first (The Joan) is created using padding, which gives extra height and volume to your hair. If you have fine hair this is the easiest version to try to help you create a huge beehive.

See page 80 for the second beehive variation.

You will need
Hairdryer
Round brush
Pin-curl clips, heated rollers or curling tongs
Comb
Section clips
Soft bristle brush for smoothing
Kirby grips
Hair padding

Step 1
Prep your hair to get volume and wave, using heated rollers, tongs or a hair dryer and pin-curl clips (Fig. 1).

Step 2
Section your hair into five parts (Fig. 2).

Section 1: the fringe.

Section 2: the top of your head to below the crown.

Section 3: the left side of your head roughly 2 cm behind your ear.

Section 4: the right side of your head roughly 2 cm behind your ear (both the left and right side are put up in the same way so will be dealt with together).

Section 5: the back of your head.

Clip all of the sections neatly away.

Step 3
Unclip the section at the top of your head and start taking smaller sections through it. Backcomb each of these small sections from the front to the back, using hairspray between sections, until the entire top section has been backcombed (Fig. 3).

* Don't be afraid to make this as big as you can. You can make it smaller when you start to secure the shape.

Step 4
Secure your hair padding into place around the crown area using Kirby grips (Fig. 4).

Step 5

Start covering the hair padding with your backcombed sections of hair, smoothing out your sections with a soft boar bristle brush as you go along (Fig. 5). Be careful not to completely brush out your backcombing.

Play around until you are happy with the shape and height of the hair that is covering the padding.

Step 6

Take the section at the back of your head and start backcombing in smaller vertical sections.

Smooth the top layer of this section and twist this hair into a French pleat leaving the ends out to style later (Fig. 6). Secure with Kirby grips.

Step 7

Secure the ends of the French pleat in a barrel curl under the hair pad with Kirby grips (Figs. 7a and 7b).

Step 8

If you have fine hair you may want to gently backcomb the sides taking sections running vertically along your head from back to front.

Smooth the sides up to where your hair padding has been placed and covered, and secure with Kirby grips, leaving the ends out to style later (Fig. 8).

Step 9

The ends of your hair now need to be styled and pinned. Secure these ends in barrel-type curls around the hair pad (Fig. 9). Be patient, sometimes this takes a bit of time.

Step 10

Release the fringe from its clip and backcomb for volume. Smooth over the layer and comb in the desired direction.

Step 11

Spray your hair with hairspray to keep it all smooth and in place.

REMEMBER!
You are probably a few inches taller now. Be careful, when you are gracefully sliding into your taxi or limo, that you don't knock your beehive out of shape.

TAKING OUT YOUR BEEHIVE

Remove all pins and hair padding.
Take a natural fibre paddle brush and gently
brush your hair starting at the very ends, working
up to the roots, until all of the backcombing has
been brushed out.

The Brigitte Beehive

The hair in a beehive wasn't always clipped completely out of the way. Emerging from the bouffant hairstyle, it also became popular for beehives to have a little bit of hair left down. Usually worn curly, this sexy style was seen on Brigitte Bardot and copied by countless fans in the sixties.

This is a softer beehive, fashioned without using a hairpiece. It is created with backcombing, which is a quicker and easier way to build a beehive, and better for thicker hair.

For a more modern style, you can backcomb your hair and smooth it just enough to give you shape, leaving you with a messy, textured beehive.

You will need
Rollers
Curling tongs
Hair ties
Comb
Hairspray
Boar bristle brush
Kirby grips

Step 1
Prep your hair using rollers or tongs for volume and wave.

Step 2
Take a diamond section of hair around your crown and tie it into a ponytail (Fig. 1). Section off the top, sides and back of the hair and clip away.

Step 3
Split the ponytail into smaller sections and start back-combing each section to create volume (Fig. 2).

Fasten the sections around the ponytail with Kirby grips to create the padding for your beehive.

Step 4
Separate the top of your hair from the sides and start to backcomb, taking sections diagonally across your head (Fig. 3). Spray with hairspray from time to time to hold.

Step 5
Smooth this section over the top of the backcombed ponytail. You can do this by rolling the section loosely over your hand and pinning the section below the ponytail with Kirby grips. Arrange the height at the top into shape and spray with hairspray to hold.

Step 6
Backcomb the sides in the same way as the top section. Smooth and pin them into place by rolling them inwards around your fingers towards the ponytail (Fig. 4). The ends from the top and sides should be tucked away, covering the original ponytail (Fig. 5). Spray with hairspray.

Step 7
Tong the ends of your hair if you prefer curly ends (this hairstyle could also look great with straight ends, if you prefer this, you could stop here).

Step 8
Pin the curled ends loosely up towards the ponytail to create a tousled look (Fig. 6). Spray with hairspray to hold.

The Jackie O Bouffant

Although this hairstyle is an icon of the sixties, it actually came into fashion in the fifties in the United States; the UK followed suit a few years later. It was designed to balance out the full-skirted shape of fifties dresses.

There was a lot of debate among fashion journalists and hairstylists in the fifties as to whether the bouffant would remain in style for long. People were concerned that it might be unflattering to their face shape and later that it was actually unhealthy to backcomb the hair so much. But Jackie Kennedy finally gave it iconic status in 1960 and it was here to stay, remaining in fashion until the end of the sixties.

The bouffant style took many different forms, it was a catch-all term for hair that was oversized and loosely coiffed.

You will need
Curling tongs
Comb
Pin tail comb
Rollers
Hairspray

Step 1
Prep your hair to create volume using heated rollers, curling tongs, or a hair dryer and pin curl clips (Fig. 1).

Step 2
Remove the rollers/clips from the curled sections around the bottom of your hairline. Start to tong these sections in reverse (away from your face) so your hair will flick up (Fig. 2).

Step 3
Backcomb this underneath section at the roots to give some root lift and smooth out.

Step 4
Remove the rest of your rollers and take a section through the middle of your head to just below the crown and start to backcomb the hair (Fig. 3). Make the hair as big as possible. Spray with hairspray to fix.

Step 5
Backcomb the sides and spray each section as before.

Step 6
Using a boar bristle brush, smooth the backcombing into shape (Fig. 4). Do this section by section, spraying each time you smooth the ends in place. Be careful not to comb out all of your backcombing. Use a pintail comb to lift areas that need to be heightened.

Step 7
Give everything a final spray with hairspray to hold.

This style looks lovely with a scarf tied as a hair band and knotted at the nape of your neck.

The Barbarella

The Barbarella is a giant wavy bouffant that is styled on long hair. A combination of the beehive and the shorter bouffant, it is often slightly tousled in style.

In the sixties, when big hair was the height of fashion, this style was featured in the adult *Barbarella* comic strip and was said to have been styled after Brigitte Bardot. Jane Fonda made the look iconic when she starred in the *Barbarella* film, which was released in 1968.

This hairstyle was a favourite of go-go dancers, with their knee high boots and miniskirts, who were first seen 'twisting' on the dance floors (and tables) of the United States in the early sixties.

You will need
Heated rollers or curling tongs
Comb
Boar bristle brush
Hair tie

Step 1

Prep your hair using heated rollers and curling tongs to give as much volume as possible and also some curl. This is a big hairstyle – don't be afraid to make it as big as you can. It's easier to pat it down and make it smaller after backcombing.

Step 2

Take a diamond-shaped section of hair through your crown area and tie this into a ponytail (Fig. 1).

Step 3

Backcomb all of the hair in the ponytail (Fig. 2).

Step 4

Secure the backcombed ponytail with Kirby grips, arranging it in a bouffant-type shape (Fig. 3). This gives the style padding and height.

Step 5

Backcomb all the hair around the ponytail to give fullness. Then smooth the top section back with a boar bristle brush to cover your ponytail padding (Fig. 4).

Step 6

Backcomb your sides and some of the curls on the ends to create extra fullness. This will also help your finished style to hold. Give it all a generous burst of hairspray.

4

To remove your style, use a boar bristle brush or paddle brush to gently smooth out the backcombing. Start from the ends of your hair and work your way up towards the roots until you have removed all of the backcombing.

How to create padding

Hair padding, also known as a 'RAT', was historically made by women using thir own hair. They would collect this from their hair brushes and put it into a hairnet or an old stocking and then use the resulting pad to create extra volume, height and support for their gravity-defying styles. Padding is particularly useful for beehive hairstyles.

Nowadays you can easily make padding using hairwefts. Or you may find a ready-made pad, in the shape you want, made out of nylon or another synthetic product at a hairdressing suppliers.

To create your own padding, you need:

❋ Hairwefts
Either made from human hair or synthetic (synthetic is usually cheaper). You can find hairwefts at any hairdressing suppliers, on the internet, or perhaps your local chemist. Try to find a hairweft the same shade as your natural hair colour. That way, if you don't manage to cover your padding completely, your hairstyle will still look fabulous.

❋ A hair net
You can usually find these in the beauty section of your local chemist.

Step 1
Double over your hair net.

Step 2
Backcomb your hairweft to give it plenty of volume and place it inside your hair net.

Step 3
Adjust it to the shape you prefer (an oval shape usually works best) and use some thin cotton to sew the edges of the hair net together. There you have it!

Introduction

It's easy to bring a touch of old-fashioned glamour back into our lives – a little decadent time spent on ourselves is an experience that everyone deserves. Looking radiant and fabulous need not be a chore, but a joy!

I aspire to the poised and ladylike allure of past decades, but that is not to say we all have to wear stockings and red lipstick (although highly recommended) – the same principles can be applied to any era. Making yourself look good makes you feel good, and make-up is one of life's little luxuries that we can always afford. The Lipstick Effect – the theory that women buy more cosmetics during hard times to cheer themselves up instead of more expensive luxury items – can be seen as far back as The Great Depression of the 1930s.

At The Powder Room, we try to bring this experience to all you deserving glamourettes. But for those we can't reach, I have put together a 'how to' guide to achieving our favourite retro looks at home. Goddess Dita Von Teese once replied in an interview, when asked what she liked least about herself, that she would never draw attention to her flaws. This is a superb rule for life, as people generally don't notice flaws unless they are pointed out. In the same way, this book is all about accentuating your best features and not worrying about flaws!

'It's your duty to be beautiful!'

Katie
X

Tips and Tools

Here are a few useful tips that we think will help you to recreate the glamour of the past, and the essential items you'll need to achieve it.

- A good skincare routine is the best place to start. Always cleanse, tone and moisturise, and NEVER go to sleep in your makeup!

- Two items you really can't skimp on are a good foundation and primer. Primer will make your foundation go on more smoothly and will help fix it all day. Make sure you get the right shade for your skin tone and that, when applied, your face looks the same colour as your neck! If you can create the best possible blank canvas, the rest of your make-up will look divine.

- If you want heavier eye make-up with dark eyeshadows, a good tip is to apply your foundation *after* finishing your eyes, as some eyeshadows can drop onto your foundation during application, spoiling all your good work.

- When doing any part of your make-up, wipe off any excess product on your brush onto the back of your hand first – it is much better to start light and build up.

- When choosing red lipsticks... generally, blue-reds suit fair, pink-toned skin, and orange-reds suit dark, yellow-toned skin. But there are exceptions to every rule, so try a few and choose what makes you feel the most fabulous.

- Finally, well-groomed eyebrows are a must. Most brows will need a little help with tweezers and make-up. It's worth it – your make-up simply doesn't look finished without!

Handy Tools

wedge sponges (non-latex)

cotton buds

essential brushes: powder, blusher, defining brush, eyeshadow brush, socket brush, blending brush, eyeliner brush, eyebrow brush, retractable lip brush for your handbag

blotting papers

false eyelashes

Capsule Make-up Bag

Whilst it is wonderful to have all the latest new products, you can achieve many looks with a relatively small amount of make-up.

foundation and primer

concealer

powder compact

three eyeshadows: pale beige shimmer, matte mid-brown, matte dark charcoal

mascara

liquid, gel or cream eyeliner and pencil eyeliner

blusher

lip pencil

lipstick

lip gloss

The following pages will show you how to recreate some iconic looks from past decades that we think are still very popular and wearable today, and can be brought up to date with a few little changes here and there. They are also the basis for many modern adaptations, so once you have mastered these simple techniques you will be a dab hand at a great many others, too!

The Looks

1920s
Clara Bow

After the Edwardian era, with its soft, delicate make-up and very long hair, and World War I, when make-up was scarce, the 1920s was a stark contrast. Particularly during the 'Roaring Twenties' – between 1925 and 1929 – dressing up, dancing and partying was a huge part of life. Icons of this period included Clara Bow, Louise Brooks and Josephine Baker – huge stars of their day, with their short bobbed haircuts and strikingly heavily made-up looks. The classic look of the flapper girls of the jazz clubs was dark, smoky kohl-rimmed eyes; long, dark eyebrows; and small, very dark-red rosebud lips.

Step 1

Start with a blank canvas – your face should be perfectly primed and ready for foundation. Apply foundation with a brush, sponge or simply fingers! Make sure you blend well and have no streaks or edges – a wedge sponge is good for this. (When doing smoky eyes, you may want to apply foundation after step 6.) Prime the eyes, and cover with a light eye concealer – some products do both these jobs in one. Lightly powder all over.

Step 2

With a very soft black or grey kohl eye pencil, line your eyes all the way around and smudge and soften the edges. You can also line the inside of the lower lid.

Step 3

Take your eyeshadow brush and coat it with your charcoal eyeshadow; gently dab off any excess on the back of your hand. Begin sparingly and, in very small circular movements, start at the outer edge of the lid and socket, and gradually blend towards the inner corner.

Step 4

Eyebrows were quite thin and dark, long and angled down. If you wish, you can just define them well with a small angled brush and a complimentary eyeshadow or a matte pencil.

You can repeat Step 3 until you get the required density. Much better to build up gradually. Use your blending brush to make sure you don't have any hard edges.

Step 5

Apply lashings of mascara to the top and bottom eyelashes.

Step 6

Apply a subtle dusting of a peachy blusher to the apples of the cheeks (find these by smiling – the apples are the parts of your cheek that rise up into a round shape).

Step 7

Line lips with pencil and apply dark red lipstick to create a well-defined small rosebud, to complete the starlet look. If you have a wider mouth you can still achieve this look, just don't take your lip line right to the corners. A neutral lip colour or gloss also suits this look and brings it more up to date.

1930s
Marlene Dietrich

The era of the silver-screen goddess, 1930s' style was very different to that of the heavy make-up and short flapper dresses of the 1920s. This was the era of the long cream silk evening gown, cut on the bias to accentuate all those curves, rather than the flattened busts of the twenties! Goddesses of the day included Marlene Dietrich, Jean Harlow and Greta Garbo, who all embodied the perfect glamour of the decade. Hair was slightly longer and softly waved, eyes were glossy in golds and champagnes to compliment those evening dresses, eyebrows were pencil-thin, long and highly arched, and lips were a lighter, softer red with a curved cupid's bow.

Step 1

Start with a blank canvas (perfectly primed), and apply your foundation. Prime the eyes and cover with a light eye concealer (some products do both these jobs in one). Apply light powder all over.

Step 2

Take your eyeshadow brush and coat it with a soft gold or champagne colour and sweep across the entire eyelid and browbone. Repeat on the other side. This should be shimmery.

Step 3

Take your socket brush and, with a very subtle neutral stone or light brown, shade in the socket. If you tilt your head down slightly you will find it easier to find the correct place to shade. You want to create a sleepy hooded eye, so don't blend too far up to the browbone.

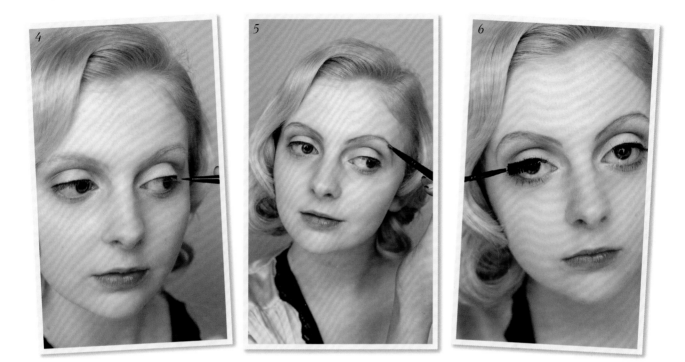

Step 4

Take your eyeliner brush and apply a thin line across the top lashes, not too extended.

Step 5

Eyebrows were extremely pencil-thin, but don't feel you need to pluck them all away! You can just define them well with a small angled brush and a complementary eyeshadow or a pencil.

Step 6

Apply lashings of mascara or, even better, a really fine, feathery set of false eyelashes (see page 100).

To achieve shiny, glossy lids, people sometimes used to apply Vaseline over their eyeshadow.

Step 7

Apply a very subtle dusting of a pale peachy blusher to the apples of the cheeks (see page 24), and more blusher evenly blended across the cheekbone. If you don't have the highly sculpted cheekbones of Marlene Dietrich, you can fake it by shading a little under your cheekbone with a darker, beigey blusher – you can find where to apply it by sucking in your cheeks!

Step 8

Finally, for an authentic look, add a soft shiny red lipstick to fully lined lips with rounded cupid's bow. Marlene would pencil outside her natural lip line to create this.

1940s
Rita Hayworth

Make-up in the 1940s was all about the lipstick — and matte red was the look. Even land girls wouldn't be seen without it! During World War II, make-up was in short supply so women became very inventive — using boot polish for mascara, for example! Women in the 1940s aspired to the Hollywood version, typified by Rita Hayworth, and although few could achieve it in such tough times, they still made the effort to be glamorous!

Step 1

As always, start with perfectly primed skin and apply your foundation and powder well – matte was the order of the day. Prime eyes, too, and use a light concealer.

Step 2

With your eyeshadow brush, apply a neutral beige colour to the whole eyelid.

Step 3

Take your socket brush and, with a very subtle neutral stone or light brown, shade in the socket. If you tilt your head down slightly you will find it easier to find the correct place to shade. You want it barely there for a daytime look, but you can go slightly darker for evening looks.

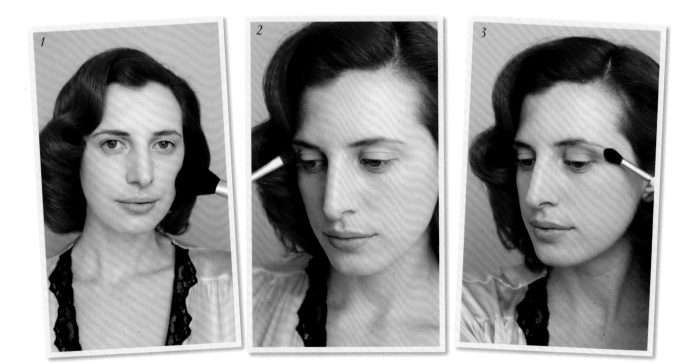

Step 4

Take a good liquid eyeliner and apply a very thin line along the eyelashes of your upper lid, from the inner towards the outer corner, and extend it slightly.

Step 5

Use an angled brush to define your eyebrows and gently accentuate the arch, in a complementary or slightly darker colour.

Step 6

Use lashings of mascara – for an authentic look, just apply to the upper lashes. For Hollywood glamour, false eyelashes are essential (see page 100).

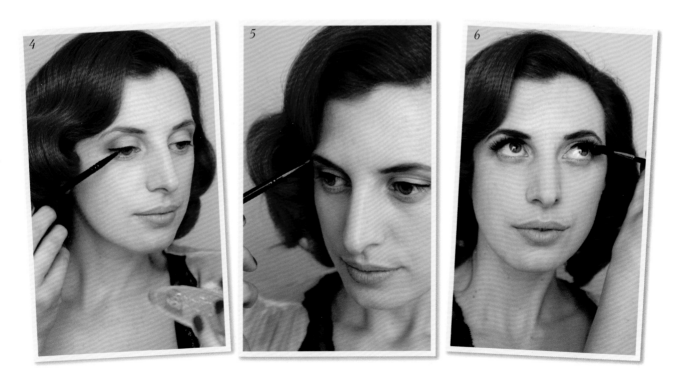

Step 7

Rouge was popular in the 1930s, so a light dusting of rosy pink to the apples will compliment this look.

Step 8

Lips need to be perfectly lined with a good red pencil that matches your lipstick, and the lipstick needs to be a very matte pillar-box red. Blot well.

1950s
Marilyn Monroe

The 1950s saw much more colour in both make-up and fashion – in fact, it was quite the done thing to match your eyeshadow to your handbag! Blues and greens or pinks and violets were popular for eyes, and corals and pinks for lips. Eyebrows were more defined and angled sharply, and tans were in fashion – fake or otherwise! Blondes were still favoured, and what better bombshell to emulate than Marilyn Monroe? A perfect cross between girl next door and sex kitten.

Step 1

As always, start with perfectly primed skin and apply your foundation. A more tanned complexion was fashionable and not too matte – so keep a little natural shine.

Step 2

With your eyeshadow brush, cover the whole eyelid up to the brow with a light, shimmery golden champagne colour.

Step 3

Take your socket brush and, in round circular movements, make a really natural socket shading with a taupe colour.

Step 4

Take your eyeshadow brush again and, with a soft coral/pink (or a blue or green), go over the eyelid from the outer corner fading to the inner corner.

Step 5

With a fine eyeliner brush, using a brown or black, take a fine line across the top lid along the lashes: tapering narrowest at the inner corner, getting thicker to the outer corner, and slightly elongate the line and flick up the end a little into a point. A good tip is to lift your chin while still looking in the mirror – this will enable you to apply the line with your eye still open, which will be much smoother than if you close one eye.

Step 6

With your angled brush, using a matte colour to compliment your eyebrows, enhance your eyebrows with short brush strokes into a sharp angle – thicker at the inner end and tapering off to a point at the outer end.

Step 7

Mascara the top lashes thickly, and the bottom ones just a little.

Step 8

Use a warm corally pink for your blusher, in round movements over the apples (see page 24), and a little up the cheekbones.

Step 9

Take a pinky red or corally red lip pencil and line your lips. They should be more rounded than a 1940s' cupid's bow but not as rounded as the 1930s' shape. Fill in with a matching lipstick – not too matte, more glossy was the look.

For a really authentic Marilyn look, you could add a beauty spot just outside your smile line, and white eye pencil inside the lower eyelid.

1960s
Audrey Hepburn

The effortlessly chic Audrey Hepburn was a classic style icon of the 1950s and 1960s. However, it was her early 1960s *Breakfast at Tiffany's* look, as Holly Golightly, that went on to inspire styles that everyone wanted to emulate. Less colour, more natural lips, heavier eye make-up, and lashings of eyeliner!

Step 1

With perfectly primed skin, apply your foundation and powder. You can even dab a little foundation on your lips with a sponge, as very nude lips were part of the look. Prime the eyes as well, and use a light concealer. Lightly powder all over the face and eyes.

Step 2

With your eyeshadow brush, apply a pale taupe colour to the whole eyelid and browbone.

Step 3

Take your socket brush, and with a very dark grey or black eyeshadow shade in the socket. If you tilt your head down slightly you will find it easier to find the correct place to shade.

Step 4

Take a good liquid, gel or cream eyeliner, and with a fine-pointed brush, apply a line along the eyelashes of your upper lid from the inner to the outer corner. You can go quite thick with this, building up gradually, but make sure it is thinner at the inner corner and goes to a point at the other end – you want the classic flick at the outer corners (see page 98). As before, if you lift your chin so that you are looking down into a mirror with both eyes just barely open, your eyelids won't screw up and you will find it easier to get a smooth line.

Step 5

Use an angled brush to define your eyebrows in a slightly darker colour. Audrey Hepburn-style eyebrows were very defined, thickened above the brow and very angled.

Step 6

Use plenty of mascara or, even better, false eyelashes (see page 100).

Step 7

You want barely there blusher in a pale colour – peaches and apricots work well. A little on the apples (see page 24) and up along the top of the cheekbone.

Step 8

Use a very natural pinkish lip colour – not too glossy but not matte.

1960s
Twiggy

A key 1960s look was that of the child-like innocence epitomised by Twiggy. Essential elements were: mini skirts and flat shoes, short neat little bobs, perfect natural complexion, nude glossy lips, and round doll-like eyes with huge eyelashes top and bottom. Although colours and flowers featured heavily towards the end of the sixties, it is the combination of monochrome clothing and heavily made-up eyes that truly embodies the 'Swinging Sixties'.

Step 1

Start with perfectly primed skin. Apply your foundation very lightly – keeping it natural. If you have freckles, embrace them and don't cover them up! Prime eyes, too, and use a light concealer. Lightly powder all over face and eyes.

Step 2

With your eyeshadow brush, apply any pastel colour or even white to the whole eyelid.

Step 3

Take your socket brush and, with a very dark grey or black eyeshadow, shade in the socket. If you tilt your head down slightly, you will find it easier to find the correct place to shade. You can blend this a little, but a really defined and arched socket line was very sixties. You can even use an eyeliner pencil if you want a really authentic look.

Step 4

Take a good liquid, gel or cream eyeliner, and with a fine-pointed brush, apply a line along the eyelashes of your upper lid from the inner to the outer corner. You can build this up gradually, but make sure it is thinner at the inner corner and goes to a point at the other end. Add the classic flick (see page 98) at the outer corners, but make it longer, much thicker and more pronounced for this look.

Step 5

For an authentic Twiggy, you will want to paint on a
few lower lashes at the outer corner of the lower lid.
Be sure to taper them off to a point and curve them
slightly.

Step 6

Use an angled brush to define your eyebrows, but
keep them very natural.

Step 7

Lashings of mascara, and false eyelashes (see page 100) are an absolute must – the thicker the better! Twiggy was famous for wearing three pairs!

Step 8

You want barely there blusher in a pale colour. Apply a little on the apples (see page 24) and carry on up along the top of the cheekbone slightly. This look was all about the eyes, so everything else was pared right down.

9

Step 9

Lips should be nude – just a very natural gloss. You could even use foundation instead of lipstick to achieve a 1960s' look.

1970s
Farrah Fawcett

The 1970s was all about looking naturally fit, glowing and healthy, à la Charlie's Angels. The perfectly tanned, toned and highlighted Farrah Fawcett was the ultimate icon of the era, with her bronzed make-up, lots of eye shadow and healthy shiny lips. But some people also loved a good splash of Studio 54 glitz and glamour for the evenings, with plenty of glitter and gloss!

Step 1

As always, start with perfectly primed skin and apply your foundation. A tanned-looking complexion is what's needed here, with a little natural shine. Powder with a slightly bronzed powder or one that has some shimmer, to add to the glowing, healthy tanned look.

Step 2

With your eyeshadow brush, use a warm golden brown or an olive green and lightly take it over the whole eyelid up to the crease.

Step 3

Take your socket brush, and with a darker bronzy brown, work in small circular movements from the outer edge of the socket line and fade out to the centre.

Step 4

With your defining brush, take a dark brown or black eyeshadow; start at the outer edge of your eye and work along the top lashes, tapering and fading off just past the centre. You want this to look like a softer, more smudgy eyeline. Repeat along the lower lash line, again tapering and fading off just past the centre.

Step 5

Apply plenty of thick mascara, and define eyebrows with a natural brown eyeshadow or pencil.

Step 6

For blusher, use an orangey brick colour or bronzer; take along the cheekbones, not onto the apples.

Step 7

Lips should be glossy and shiny.

1980s
Siouxie Sioux

Punk was a huge scene in the 1970s and early 1980s, with Siouxie Sioux being someone you could aspire to look like or just dip into now and again as part of your own mini-rebellion. This is quite a dramatic look and not for the faint-hearted! The overall effect is very sharp and angular. You can, of course, pare this right down; leaving out her trademark eyebrows and shortening the eyelines would make it much more wearable. The eyeliner could be much finer, and you don't have to have such a pale face!

Step 1

Start with perfectly primed skin and apply your foundation and powder well (this was a matte look). Keep your complexion pale, but not paler than your neck. Prime eyes, too, and use a light concealer. As this look has lots of dark, heavy eyeshadow, you may want to apply your foundation later (after step 3).

Step 2

Take your eyeshadow brush and load it up with a light, matte, neutral colour and take this all over the lid up to the brow. This is just to help you blend later.

Step 3

Apply a black eyeshadow all over the eyelid and into the socket line, building up the intensity as you go but taking care not to go into the inner hollow against the nose. Take your blending brush and blend up towards the browbone and out towards the temples, making sure you have no edges.

Step 4

With your eyeliner brush, load up with black liquid, gel or cream eyeliner and, as with the 1960s, take it along the lash line of the top lid from inner corner to outer. For authenticity, you can extend this right down to the inner corner and onto the nose, and also elongate it at the outer corner towards the temples. Again, build up the thickness gradually.

Step 5

With the same eyeliner brush, follow the lower lash line from inner to outer (this line is not as thick as the top line). Extend the line on to the nose, parallel with the upper line, leaving a gap in between. Join up with the top line at the outer corner. Fill in the gap at the inner corner with a white pencil.

Step 6

Apply plenty of thick mascara.

Step 7

With the black eyeshadow, take your angled brush and start to work into the eyebrows. The shape is not a natural one – it is very thick and straight-edged, tapering down along the nose and elongated outwards towards the temple.

Step 8

No blusher is needed for this look – just a little shading with a brown eyeshadow to enhance the cheekbones (see page 32).

Step 9

Lips had a very pointed cupid's bow, and were in a very dark glossy red.

1980s
Madonna

The 1980s was a 'more is more' era. Whether it was money, power or hair and make-up, everything was big! Lots of eye make-up, coloured mascara, strong blusher and frosted, metallic lip shades. What with so much power-dressing, inspired by films like *Working Girl*, and the rich and immaculately polished looks of 'Dynasty' and 'Dallas', it was no wonder that the devil-may-care Madonna was a breath of fresh air! The remnants of Punk became softer, merging into the pop scene – and the looks of *Desperately Seeking Susan* and 'Like a Virgin' were copied everywhere.

Step 1

Start with perfectly primed skin, and apply a good coverage foundation (use concealer and powder well). This wasn't a 'natural' look.

Step 2

Take a good orangey eyeshadow, and lightly dust it all over the eyelid. Concentrate the colour to the outer corner of the eyelid and into the socket, fading out slightly towards the inner corner and brow (or use a yellowy gold in the inner corner).

Step 3

With a darker eyeshadow, take a little of this along the top lashes – it should be thicker at the outer corner, fading out after the centre. Repeat along the bottom lashes.

Step 4

You can intensify this with a pencil to get a stronger look, provided you have a smudger, so you can blend it out.

Step 5

Apply plenty of mascara. Lots of mascara was fashionable in the 1980s.

Step 6

Eyebrows were 'natural' and brushed upwards. Don't feel you have to grow yours for this look, just give them a good brush upwards and you will have an eighties feel!

Step 7

Use an orangey brick colour blusher, and apply it right along the edge of the cheekbone and into the hollow underneath, to give a bit of shading.

Step 8

Lipsticks were generally very metallic and shimmery in the 1980s but, for this look, Madonna wore an orangey red lipstick.

Extras

Fabulous Flicks

One thing that people often find difficult to do themselves is applying liquid eyeliner, especially with a vintage-style flick-up at the ends. Here are a few tips that will help you, but practise makes perfect! You will need a compact mirror so you can get up close, and it is usually much easier to use a really good eyeliner brush rather than the applicator that comes with the product. You may also find a cream or gel eyeliner easier to use than a liquid, as it is a bit easier to control.

1. Dip your brush into your chosen eyeliner, and make sure it is well coated. Wipe off the excess on the back of your hand, spinning the brush so as to make it into a good point.
2. Take your compact mirror and hold it slightly lower down. Raise your chin so your eyes are almost closed – this will allow you to keep both eyes open. If you close one eye, it tends to screw up slightly and you won't get a smooth line.
3. If you don't feel confident to do a line in one sweep, start in the middle and take the line out to the outer corner. You can keep going over this, each time edging gradually further towards the inner corner.
4. Try not to pull your eyelid taut, as this can distort the line. You want to keep your eyelid in as natural a position as possible so you can see exactly where to put the line.
5. You want your line to finely taper off at the inner corner and get thicker towards the outer corner, tapering off upwards into a flick.
6. Make sure the flick is a smooth curve rather than a tick. A good rule of thumb is to follow the curve of your lower lid as if you were extending that curve.

Luscious Lashes

False eyelashes have had something of a resurgence in recent years, and can really enhance your make-up. These days, you can have semi-permanent individual lashes attached to your own lashes for a really natural look, which is hard to detect even close up. But this is time-consuming and expensive, and you can't do this yourself at home – so here are some tips for you to try yourself.

Full-strip lashes

These give the most dramatic effect, although you can get some quite thin and natural strips. They usually come with their own glue, but if they don't you will need to get a latex-based eyelash glue.

1. Before you glue the lashes on, measure them for size along your own lashes. The longest lashes are for the outside edge of your eye. If they are too wide, cut them down lash by lash from the outside edge until they are the right width for you.
2. Squeeze out some of the glue on to the back of your hand; don't squeeze directly on to the lashes, and never directly on to your eyelid.
3. Run the lashes through the glue so that there is an even amount of glue all along the lash.
4. Blow onto the glue on the lashes, or leave them for several seconds. This allows the glue to start to set and become more tacky, which will make it much easier and quicker to fix them in place.
5. Once tacky, close one eye without screwing it up (raising your eyebrows helps to keep the skin smooth) and place the lashes outer-edge first as close to your own lashes as possible. Gently press into place with your fingertips or a cotton bud, paying particular attention to the corners. (Some people will use tweezers at this point but, if you do, please make sure you are not in danger of your hand slipping or anyone jogging you. Sharp, pointy things near the eye is never a good thing!)
6. Repeat on the other side, and then blend any edges with some liquid eyeliner.

Half-strip Lashes

You can buy half-length strip lashes or you can cut the full length ones in half. This look really suits and enhances a 1950s' flicked eyeline. Apply half-strip lashes in the same way as the full strip, fixing to the outer corner first.

Individual Lashes

You can buy either single lashes or lashes in a group of three or more, fanning out from a single point. Both come in different lengths and look very natural. This process is quite fiddly to do, so you may want a friend to help you.

1. You will probably only want to apply four or five individual lashes to each eye, so pick them out and line them up for each eye before you start. You want the longest ones for the outer corners, getting shorter as you move along the lash line towards the centre. You may only want them to go as far as the centre, as they look more obvious towards the inner corner.
2. Squeeze the glue on to the back of your hand as before and, taking the longest lash, dip the bulb into the glue and allow it to dry slightly.
3. Place the lash right into the lash line at the outer corner.
4. Repeat along the lash line, spacing well. Make sure you put them in at the same angle as your natural lashes, otherwise they could all stick out at different angles – looking rather too spidery!

Beautiful Brows

Because eyebrows were so defining of an era – from the pencil-thin brows of the 1930s to the natural, bushy brushed-up eyebrows of the 1980s – it is rather too drastic to actually change them for a particular make-up look. Retro looks are all about a nod towards an era rather than slavishly following a look. Keeping them tidy and groomed will complete any look perfectly. There are plenty of brow bars these days where you can get them professionally threaded or waxed, but it's so simple to just pluck them yourself at home.

You will need a really good pair of tweezers – quality really does matter in this instance. Slant-edged are easiest to use and they need to be sharp, but not so sharp as to cut the hairs. To ensure your tweezers keep a good grip on the hairs, regularly wipe the tips. Please try to avoid over-plucking – it can take an age for brows to grow back!

1. Make sure that you're near a window – daylight is quite unforgiving and will show up everything! Magnifying mirrors can really help, as you can see each hair very clearly, but keep checking the entire look in a standard mirror.
2. The space between your brows should not be too wide. To find where your brow should start, take a make-up brush and hold it parallel to the side of your nose. Where the brush meets your brow is where your brow should begin. You can get a good idea of where to end the length of your brow by extending the brush diagonally from your nostril to the outside edge of your eye.
3. Most brows look best with a slight arch. To know where to make this, hold the brush parallel to the outside edge of the iris to see where the highest part of the arch should be.
4. Proceed with caution and stop every few hairs to look at the whole shape. Pluck hairs one at a time, and in the direction they grow. You may find it easier and less painful if you hold the skin taut.
5. When you have achieved your desired shape, brush through your brows. You can apply something soothing like a toner to calm any redness and help close the pores.
6. If your brows are sparse or have gaps, you can fill them in by brushing a matte brown eyeshadow using an angled brush or an eyeliner pencil. Use short strokes in the direction of the hairs to make them look as if they are real hairs.
7. For unruly, wayward eyebrows, a dab of gel smoothed through or a little hairspray sprayed onto a brow brush and brushed through will help them stay put!

Marvellous Manicures

A good manicure will finish off your look perfectly, so taking care of your hands and nails is an important part of your beauty routine. A really cheap and easy way to get smooth hands is to rub them with a mixture of almond oil and sugar and then rinse in warm water; this exfoliates and moisturises them at the same time. If your cuticles need work, soak your hands in warm water first for at least five minutes, to soften the cuticles. Massage in some cuticle oil, and push the cuticles back gently using a soft rubber hoof stick rather than an orange stick – this will avoid causing any damage to the cuticle. This is much better for your cuticles than than trimming or cutting them.

Now your hands are prepped, you will need the following: nail polish remover, cotton wool pads, cotton buds, nail file (not metal), nail buffer, base coat, colour and top coat.

1. Firstly, remove any old nail polish. Soak a cotton pad in nail polish remover; press onto nail and hold for several seconds, and then gently rub away from the skin around the nail until all traces of the old nail polish have been removed.
2. Take your nail file and file nails to the desired shape; oval shapes tend to suit most people. File in one direction only using the coarse side of the emery board to shorten and shape the nail, and then smooth the edge with the finer side.
3. If your nails have ridges or are uneven, you can smooth them with a nail buffer, starting with the roughest side and ending with the smoothest side.
4. Use a cotton wool pad with some nail polish to wipe over the nails to get rid of any dust from filing and buffing, or any oil that would prevent the nail polish 'sticking' correctly.
5. Always use a base coat – it provides a smooth surface for polish and prevents nail polish from staining the nails. Apply one coat: one stroke of polish down the middle, then one on either side of the nail. Try not to keep going over each stroke.
6. Apply two coats of your colour in the same way, taking care not to stray onto the cuticle or skin around the nail.
7. Top coats add shine and help your manicure last longer without chipping, especially if you re-apply everyday. Apply one coat in the same manner.
8. You can correct any straying bits of nail polish around your nails or cuticles with a cotton bud dipped in to nail polish remover, or better still there are some great corrector pens on the market!

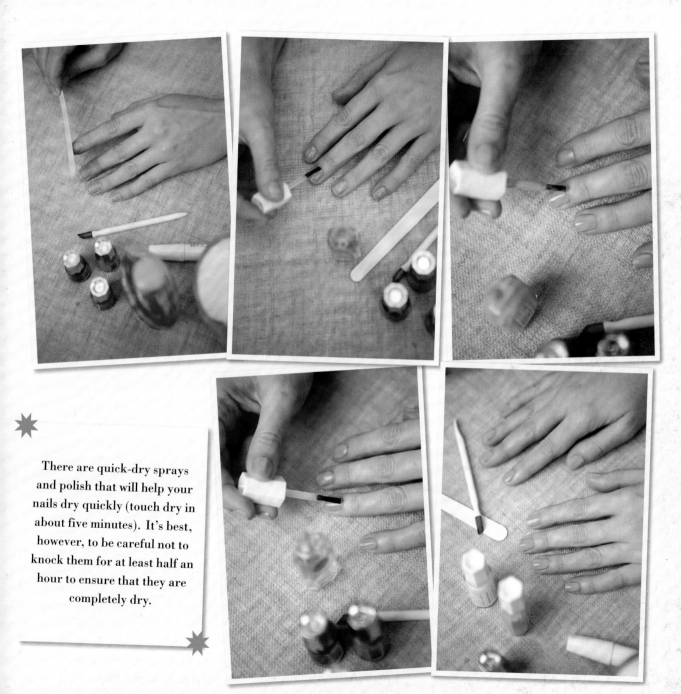

There are quick-dry sprays and polish that will help your nails dry quickly (touch dry in about five minutes). It's best, however, to be careful not to knock them for at least half an hour to ensure that they are completely dry.

1940s-style Manicure

Fashions in nails have changed as much as fashions in make-up – not just colours, but shapes and methods. But the most strikingly different of them all was the 1940s' manicure with bare moons. This was when nails were meticulously painted so as to leave the half-moon shape at the bed of the nail by the cuticle free from colour. It is a beautiful look, but it does tend to foreshorten the nail, so looks best on longer oval-shaped nails. This is quite tricky to do yourself!

1. Start as you would a standard manicure – taking care of your hands and cuticles, and shaping the nail into an oval shape.
2. Paint your nails with a base coat as normal.
3. Using a red, if you wish to be traditional, paint your nails in the normal way, but trying as best as you can not to paint onto the half-moons at all. You can try to achieve the shape now, but don't worry if it looks a bit messy at this point!
4. Do a second coat of colour in the same method.
5. Then take a fine-pointed make-up brush (such as an eyeliner brush), dip it in some nail polish remover and, using this, you can tidy up any bits of colour that have strayed onto the moons and neaten up the arch shape. But take care to wipe the brush every time you use it, or you will end up with streaky moons!
6. When you are happy with all the shapes, add your top coat.

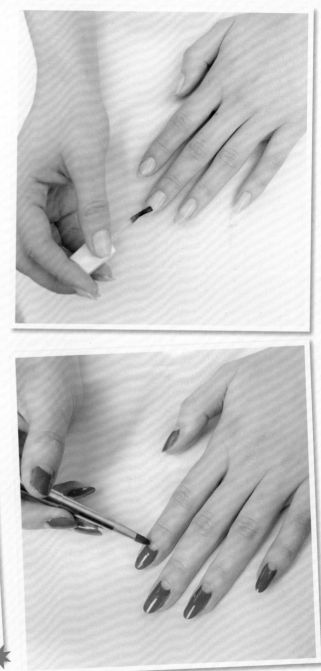

If you find this very difficult, you can try using the arch-shaped stickers you find in French manicure kits – just use them at the base instead of the tips. If you go down this route, make sure you wait until the polish is completely dry before you remove the stickers, so as not to smudge them.

Glossary

Blending brush – thick and round with a soft, angled top.
Blotting papers – small fine tissues for blotting shiny patches.
Blusher brush – smaller round, dome-shaped or softly tapered brush.
Defining brush – very short and very dense, round and pointed.
Eyebrow brush – stiff, very small, flat, straight-edged, angled brush.
Eyeliner – for flicks, liquid, gel or cream liner works best (liquid is wettest, so some people find cream or gel easier to use). For smudgey or smokey looks a soft Kohl pencil is best.
Eyeliner brush – very thin and pointed.
Eyeshadow brush – short, flat, curved top and fluffy.
Hoof stick – angled soft rubber end for pushing back cuticles.
Powder brush – large round, dome-shaped brush.
Retractable lip brush – pointed brush that retracts into itself, with a lid.
Smudger – tapered foam end for softening eyeliner.
Socket brush – soft, slim, long and tapered.

Clothes Picture credits

Images ©: 23: Blue Lantern Studio / Corbis; 31: V&A Images / Alamy; 33T: AF archive / Alamy; 33B: Pictorial Press Ltd / Alamy; 43: Mary Evans Picture Library / National Magazine Company 53: Jeff Morgan 09 / Alamy; 57: Ken Sparkes; 63: V&A Images / Alamy; 73: Condé Nast Archive/Corbis; 83: Condé Nast Archive / Corbis; 87: Glenn Harvey / Alamy; 100: Celine Chapman; 108: Anthony Lycett

Hair Picture credits

ALAMY: p.50 Photos 12/Alamy; p.64© Mary Evans Picture Library/Alamy; p.84 © Interfoto/Alamy; p.85 © Photos 12/Alamy; p.92 © Pictorial Press Ltd/Alamy ALAN HUTCHINGS PHOTOGRAPHY: pp. 1, 2, 3, 20, 27, 30, 36, 41, 44, 49, 52, 55, 58, 63, 66, 69, 71, 74, 79, 80, 86, 90, 91, 94, 97 CORBIS: p.18 © Hulton-Deutsch Collection/Corbis; p.28 (left) © Underwood & Underwood/Corbis; p.29 © Rune Hellestad/Corbis; p.34 © Underwood & Underwood/Corbis; p.35 © Bettmann/Corbis; p.42 © Bettmann/Corbis; p.43 © Bettmann/Corbis; p.51 © Stephane Cardinale/People Avenue/Corbis; p.56 © Bettmann/Corbis; p.57 © Sara De Boer/Retna Ltd/Corbis; p.65 © Eric Thayer/Reuters/Corbis; p.72 (left) © Sunset Boulevard/Corbis; p.72 (centre) © John Springer Collection/Corbis; p.73 © A3508 Rolf Vennenbernd/dpa/Corbis; p.100 © Bettmann/Corbis; GETTY IMAGES: p.19 © Jason Squires/Getty Images; p.93 © Karl Prouse/Getty Images; p.101 © Carlos Alvarez/Getty Images JOHN ANGUS: pp. 4, 7, 16, 17, 19, 29, 35, 43, 51, 57, 65, 73, 85, 93, 98, 99, 101, 102, 104, 106, 109 MARY EVANS PICTURE LIBRARY: p.28 (centre) © Mary Evans Picture library

Make-up Picture credits

Clothes Acknowledgements

Thanks to Katherine Higgins, Angel Adoree, Olly and Jess from the Vintage Emporium, Ian and Ian from Hunky Dory Vintage, Emily Preece-Morrison at Anova and Rebecca Winfield for all your help and support. Thank you to The Vintage Mafia for being the best friends a gal could wish for.

Hair Acknowledgements

Thanks are due to our shoot assistants Dominique Rigby and Catherine Losing; Cosima and the staff of All Star Bowling Lanes, London E1; and the following shops who kindly lent vintage clothing and props: Vintage Mode, Grays Antique Market, London W1; Linda Bee, Grays Antique Market, London W1; Annie's, Camden Passage, London N1; This Shop Rocks, London E1; Vintage Store, London E1; and stylist Susan Downing, who loaned items from her private collection.

The publishers would also like to thank Belinda and the staff of The Painted Lady vintage and contemporary hairstyling salon. www.thepaintedladylondon.com

Make-up Acknowledgements

Thanks to

The Powderpuff Girls team
Paul & Joe Beauté
Lola
The Balm
T.LeClerc
Mavala
Mum and Dad x

First published in the United Kingdom in 2012 by
PAVILION BOOKS
10 Southcombe Street, London W14 0RA
An imprint of Anova Books Company Ltd

Commissioning editor: Emily Preece-Morrison; Nina Sharman
Designer: Georgina Hewitt
Photographer: Christina Wilson; Caroline Molloy
Hair and make-up stylist: Lipstick and Curls; Belinda Hay; Luisa Savoia;
Katie Reynolds; Bethany Swan, Dominika Kasperowicz
Clothing stylist: Naomi Thompson; Susan Downing; Heather MacVean
Models: Fleur De Guerre, Annie Smith, Teowa, Gemma King, Kezia Argue, Lisa Prest,
Rachel Baynton, Jennifer Siggs, Alice Saggers, Laura Lee, Hazel Holtham, Bethan Garland,
Annie Andrews, Harriet Thompson, Siren Stiletto, Jaime McLennan, Jessica de Lotz, Bao Reinke,
Jo Heygate, Rebecca Johnson, Hannah Maxwell, Leah Ward, Sophia St Villier, Jasmin Paynter,
Miss Betsy Rose, Alex Grindley, Zara Sparkes, Fifi Fatale, Maia Smillie

ISBN: 9781862059764

A CIP catalogue record for this book is available from the British Library.

10 9 8 7 6 5 4 3 2 1

Colour reproduction by Mission Productions Ltd, Hong Kong
Printed and bound by 1010 Printing International, Ltd., China

www.anovabooks.com